IT
IS NOT
NOW

Books by John Gould

New England Town Meeting
Pre-natal Care for Fathers
Farmer Takes a Wife
The House That Jacob Built
And One to Grow On
Neither Hay nor Grass
Monstrous Depravity
The Parables of Peter Partout
You Should Start Sooner
Last One In
Europe on Saturday Night
The Jonesport Raffle
Twelve Grindstones
The Shag Bag
Glass Eyes by the Bottle
This Trifling Distinction
Next Time Around
No Other Place
Stitch in Time
The Wines of Pentagoët
Old Hundredth
There Goes Maine!
Funny About That
It Is Not Now

With F. Wenderoth Saunders
The Fastest Hound Dog in the State of Maine

With Lillian Ross
Maine Lingo

IT
IS NOT
NOW
Tales of Maine

JOHN GOULD

Down East Books

Camden, Maine

Down East Books

An imprint of The Rowman & Littlefield Publishing Group, Inc.
4501 Forbes Blvd., Ste. 200
Lanham, MD 20706
www.rowman.com

Distributed by NATIONAL BOOK NETWORK

British Library Cataloguing in Publication Information available

Library of Congress Cataloging-in-Publication Data available

Library of Congress Control Number: 2021933643

ISBN 978-1-60893-745-5 (paperback)
ISBN 978-1-60893-700-4 (e-book)

♾™ The paper used in this publication meets the minimum requirements of
American National Standard for Information Sciences—Permanence of Paper for
Printed Library Materials, ANSI/NISO Z39.48-1992.

For Elizabeth Mary Burke
a/k/a and d/b/a
Becky
(Grandson William's Bride)

Contents

CONTENTS

Peter Partout's Page

Dear Mr. Editor: Charlie Kierstead was sound asleep and his wife punched him in the ribs and said, "Chuck, if'n I was to die and you was to get married again, would you let your new wife drive my car?" Chuck said, "Gawd, no! She can't handle a stick shift. Now, go back to sleep!" I offer this at this time because I think it has something to do with the way things change as we go along.

(Signed) Peter Partout—Peppermint Corner

It Is Not Now

It is not now as it hath been of yore—
    Turn wheresoe'er I may,
        By night or day,
The things which I have seen I now can see no more.

                —William Wordsworth, "Ode: Intimations
                of Immortality from Recollections of
                Early Childhood"*

---

*The *Ode on Immortality* is the high water mark which the intellect has reached in this age.
                                —Ralph Waldo Emerson, 1856

IT
IS NOT
NOW

1 Longwinded Introduction

When Sim Turner came into the house for noonin' that day, his wife was standing by the cookstove ready to dish up the beans, and she said, "Ted Hunter called." Sim went to the sink, soaped his hands, and began to wash up. Thinking he hadn't heard her, she said again, "Ted Hunter called!" Sim turned to say, "Did he call twice?"

So there was this other day when I came in and my wife said, "A man from the telephone company called." This seemed to me to be a statement worth meditation. Why shouldn't a man from the telephone company call? On the other hand, why didn't he send a messenger on horseback? My wife, who knows the Ted Hunter story from away back, and is also accustomed to me, saw my hesitation and said, "He just called once."

"What-d he want?" I asked.

"Said they wanted permission to cut some bushes—the new neighbor wants a telephone. I told him to call again at twelve-fifteen."

He didn't call again.

Then I fell to wondering about this request to cut bushes. Since when did the telephone company come around and ask permission? Everybody knows that if God was standing in the way, They'd shove Him aside and cut. Eminent domain stuff. Seems odd. But he didn't call again, anyway.

My greatest asset has been people. They've been my success

and I love 'em all. I was still in high school when I learned the
value of everybody, and people are the best friends I've had. I
was in high school when I began writing the weekly page from
the town of Freeport for the Brunswick *Record*, Mr. Tobey, the
editor, told me, "I want to know what happens, and I want to
know who did it." He was a wise editor. Names are news and
will sell papers. I began dealing in Freeport names—people—
until Mr. Tobey was sending me as much as seven dollars a
week. That was a lot of money in 1924, and utter prosperity for
a boy still in school. By the time I was ready for college I had
added other papers to my string, and editors in Boston and New
York would send me more money for one story than Mr. Tobey
paid me for running all over Freeport. I learned that names—
people—are even more important than news. Well, I'd do an
item that Mr. and Mrs. Perley Fickett took supper Tuesday at
the Falmouth Hotel in Portland. This was news. But sometimes
Mr. and Mrs. Perley Fickett didn't do anything that could be
called news, and then I would write, "Mr. and Mrs. Perley Fickett stayed home Saturday evening and had popcorn." This was
not news, but it sold the paper. Mr. Nichols, who owned the
Brunswick *Record*, used to wag his head and say, "The *Record*
makes money in spite of us!" Mr. Tobey would smile. Years after
my apprenticeship with the *Record*, a New York *Times* review of
my book said, "He writes about Maine." Not so; I write about
Maine people. I owe them everything. I'd be a pauper today if
'twarn't for folks like Ted Hunter. I love them all. Perhaps I have
a knack with them.

Some say it isn't easy. When we came to our retirement years
and decided to live by tidewater in the lobster-fishing town of
Friendship, any number of people told me I would always be a
highlander. Coastal folks are clannish and standoffish, I was told,
and I'd always be "from away." They were wrong. I think back
on the first true Friendshippers I came to know. I started with
Carlton Simmons, who was the postmaster, and anybody who
ever smelled printer's ink knows a postmaster is the place to
start. Carlton was building a sloop, so I asked him about a lum-

beryard where I could buy stock for my woodworking. Carlton told me not only where to go, but where not to go—information to be appreciated. Next, I shook hands with Harold Jameson, lobsterman, who wanted to know if I was "down for the sum- muh?" Harold still asks me that every time we meet. Harold also asked me if I'd like to go haul? Until he sold his boat and retired, I would go down the bay with him a couple of times a summer to watch him handle his traps. The first time we went, we left Friendship harbor before daylight, and were below McGee Island when the sun came up and dripped great globs of red back into the ocean. There was never a more beautiful morning, and I remember it and think about all the unfortunate people in this world who have never been invited to go haul by a friendly Friendship fisherman who is a good friend. Then I met Virgil Richards, who calls Harold "Cappy." Virgil asked us to go "pleasurin' " down to one of the islands for a Sunday picnic, and he'd "save out" a pail of shedders. Otter Island, he said, made a good place.

When I met Stanley Simmons, I asked him, "Do you think they'll have it?" Stanley said, "Oh, yes—they come not ten min- utes ago and borrowed ten fathom of rope." None of my high- lander cronies had done better with a "have-it" answer in fifty years—no wonder I cherish Stanley and the friendship that came with him. Then I got acquainted with Tom Delano.

Tom, lobsterman all his years, had just had a bit of luck. He was hauling, and when he rove his warp through the snatch- block his boat was drawn right down by the side. He was "hung down" for fair, and whatever was afoul of his gear wasn't about to be started. He hailed another lobsterman, and even two "wenches" couldn't budge the line. Then something let go, and they found a seven-hundred-pound bluefin tuna had somehow become snagged in Tom's line and had done what no fish should ever do—had drowned. They boated the fish and at the Friend- ship wharf Virgil Richards dressed it for market. Then Tom took it in his pick-up truck to Rockland and got a pretty penny from the Jordan Fish Market.

When he got home he told his wife about this good fortune, and she said, "Didn't you bring none home? I'd just love to stick a tooth into a good piece of fresh tunny!"

Tom hadn't thought about that, so he drove back to Rockland and told them at Jordan's Market that he was back to buy a slice of the tuna they'd just bought from him. Jordan laughed and said nobody ought to pay for a piece of his own fish, and gave a slice to Tom.

About that time the wire lobster trap had been accepted. The ancient wooden traps were becoming obsolete, and I realized that in another decade Friendship would have plenty of youngsters who wouldn't know what a wooden trap looked like. I went to Dave Kenniston's over in Warren and bought "stock" for an old-time wooden trap and nailed one together. This one was for looks rather than the ocean, so I sand-papered the wood and gave it three coats of polyurethane. Then I took it to Tom, and he "mashed" twine for the heads and tied them into the funny-eyes just as he had equipped thousands of his own traps in a lifetime of fishing. You can see that true, old-time, wooden, one-bedroom, Muscongus Bay lobster trap in the Friendship Museum—set aside so the future can see it, and proof that a highlander can be palsy with a standoffish salt-water native. Tom and I will share the gratitude of posterity.

Coming to Friendship was good for me. Writing is a curious trade and remains esoteric. I need exposure to people, since what else would I write about?—and Friendship has the finest kind. Wordsworth told us that poetry has its origin in emotion recollected in tranquillity, and it has been my privilege to use the composure and serenity of Friendship Back River to spark my kind of doggerel. Our little home off the main road and just up from the clam flats is a comfortable place to live and work. No— we're not isolated and remote. Tourists from Indiana can find me—this is a first visit to Maine and they'd like to say hello. I have no idea what tourists do with zucchini squash, but they drive away with a bushel of mine in their back seats. Bless them!

Once I began to notice a young lady who drove down our road to the shore every so often, and she didn't look like a tourist. Then I noticed her pick-up truck had the logo of the Maine Department of Marine Resources on the door, and I was curious. Next time she came in I was waiting when she drove out, and I asked her if she'd like a cucumber. She said she came once a week to take a sample of ocean water, and the lab over at Juniper Point made an analysis for purity and, alack!, pollution. She said, "I see you got a new neighbor down to the show-wer!"

"Eyah," I said.

"From away?"

"Eyah."

Then one morning this young lady drove down, and then came right back up again. I surmised the reason, and when she came back that afternoon I had some cucumbers ready, and I said, "You missed the tide!"

"Eyah. Had to come back!"

"Thanks," I said. "I can use that!" It was comical to realize the Maine Department of Marine Resources had finally learned that our tide ebbs and flows twice in every twenty-four hours.

So the new neighbor she mentioned is the one who is getting a telephone, and it was the next day that I received a magnificent visitation, in person, from the illustrious gentleman who had called in the first place about trimming bushes. I was turning a chair leg on my shop lathe, meditating in tranquillity at the same time, when this dapper, suave, dressed-up stranger let himself in without a bit of help from anybody, and the minute I saw him I realized he had been with me three seconds too long already. He was that kind of a thing. I report only the facts. He smiled a wide Dale Carnegie smile, handed me a business card, and extended his hand. "I'm from the telephone company," he said.

I bowed, feigned enormous affability, and said, "Good for you! Let's you and me be friends!"

This invitation seemed to amuse him, confirming my original

impression, and I could see that he took no interest in being a friend. He would rather be the telephone company. He got right down to business.

He said the folks in the new cottage had requested a telephone and added, ". . . of course, we have to give them one."

"That sounds to me like a reasonable consequence," I said.

"Yes," he said.

He opened a briefcase and found some legal-looking documents which he consulted briefly and explained that "we" plan to trim some bushes in order to supply this urgent want. I decided that the telephone company, somehow, was in a sling.

I was right.

I found that when the electric power company and the telephone company put up a line to service our little home and paradise, nobody had foreseen a possible extension down over the hill, beyond. Flourishing his spurious legal documents, this paragon of gentility told me I was no longer in possession of any rights in this matter, that I didn't count any longer around here, and that my sylvan glade and bosky dell, so precious to my happiness, was forfeit to the whims of Mother Bell and associates. I had been thinking, so what? A couple of wires in the air—why not? But he threatened me, made light of my recorded deed, and smiled as he outlined my subservience to his necessity.

Well, all right . . . When you like people and have friends, there are no great disturbances. Wander over for a game of cribbage and neighbor. Henry Dolloff used to say, "Don't never ask a good Mainer to do some work for you. What you do is ask if he'll do you a favor, and he'll be right over." I haven't seen this telephone fellow since. My back up, I told him to get lost, and he went away while I finished my chair leg and recollected in tranquillity. The next thing I knew a lawyer for the electric power company became cat's-paw for the telephone folks, and began giving me a hard time about who owned my land, anyway. It seems the two utilities share poles, and the second one got mad at me because I was mad at the first one.

The sad tale is already overlong. I was minding my own business, content and relaxed. All at once I was called nothing more than a resident taxpayer to be trespassed against. I got a letter saying that I should not feel imposed upon because I am abused. After all, these big companies operate with the complete sanction of the Maine Public Utilities Commission. Think of that! I saw no way to accommodate this situation in my usual manner. How would I give zucchinis to the telephone company? Cucumbers to the power people?

We set up housekeeping in October of 1932, and since then I have paid the power company its monthly bill on time and in full. I paid for a telephone before that, and have been prompt every month. It was sad for me to realize that this meant nothing. Both companies were ready and willing to sell me, a good Mainer, down the corporate river with haughty disdain and take up cozy-like with a total stranger from out-of-state who would be here at least three weekends every August. And people come and ask me if I've noticed any changes in our—my—State of Maine. Without a qualm they were ready to cut me off!

Changes? Our Maine people haven't changed all that much. As I think back on the Freeporters whose names I fitted into my weekly *Record* letter, they come to life even though they are all long gone. Every morning they'd be at the post office—Levi Patterson, Roy Marston, Ern Pinkham, Sam Fitts, George Bartol, Dr. Lewis, Jim Cushing, Bob Randall, Win Fogg, Ike Skillin. And L. L. Bean. They shaped up as honest State-o'-Mainers. And today I see other honest State-o'-Mainers at our Friendship post office. For every Elmer Porter there is, I suppose, a Harlan Wallace, although Friendship hasn't yet produced an L. L. Bean.

Back in the 1920s we had a lawyer in Freeport, Bertram Peacock. Every morning on his way to his office in the Oxnard Block he would pause in front of Artie Mitchell's newspaper store and run a finger into the coin return slot of the pay telephone. Now and then he would find a nickel. One day Gorm Leavitt came into Squire Peacock's office and asked what he should do about

Neddie Crandell, who was stealing his hens. Squire Peacock listened to Gorm's tale of woe, then touched his fingers together across his chest, and spoke in this fashion:

"Gorm [he said], I can see you're abused and need satisfaction. Now, my fee is five dollars, and I'll take it come fall in potatoes. My advice is this—you don't need no lawyer. What you need is a friend who's handy with his fists."

That's downright for our enlightened times, but in his day Squire Peacock was accounted a fine old State-o'-Mainer.

2 Modern Thoreaux

As the *annies labuntur* Bill and I have noticed a rising wonder in the families about the wisdom of letting two old fogies wander off into the deep Maine woods without somebody to watch over them. The rigors of the uncharted wilderness where bears lurk and a thousand dangers beset in every direction! So far Bill and I have been allowed to go, and so far we have come home intact. Bill and I share two grandsons, and in the beginning our "somewhat" fishing trip was meant to get us acquainted before his daughter married my son. Our purpose was thoroughly cultural and academic, but we dissembled about fishing to give our retreat respectability.

The first summer, we set up a tent and cooked on a campfire at Baker Lake. This is far up behind the chains on logging roads, in Township 7, Range 17, and the outlet of Baker Lake is usually considered the source of the St. John River, which flows some 330 miles before finding the Bay of Fundy. Baker Lake is closer to Canada than it is to the United States, and Bill and I got there to enjoy the wilderness only with a road pass from the paper company. One evening as we sat by the fire holding scholarly discourse on the tenets of Epictetus, our pre-prandial colloquy was interrupted by the arrival of a dusty sedan bearing Felix and Velma Fernald.

Felix always boasted that he was the homeliest man ever to work for the Great Northern Paper Company—he was in the office of the area depot at Pittston Farm, just upstream from Seboomook Lake on the West Branch of the Penobscot. Velma, being perhaps the prettiest lady on the company roster, was the telephone operator at Pittston Farm. They had driven up the dirt logging road to see how we were making out. As soon as Felix saw that our intentions were wholly directed toward cultural uplift, and our purpose was to bring refinement to the upper townships, he made arrangements for us to use a company camp in the future, so for the succeeding twenty-seven summers (so far) we have not bothered with a tent. The camp is at the outlet of Caucomagomac Lake, which is pronounced cock-m'-gom-mick in full but is simply Cauc Lake in short. Henry David Thoreau was there, but called it Saint Johns Lake because he couldn't spell Caucomagomac. The camp is reasonably splendid—tight, well equipped. It has LP gas, so we have lamps, range, and refrigerator, and the beds are cozy with foam mattresses. We are not in rugged and severe circumstances to cause our families concern. We are, all the same, surrounded by wilderness. And that wilderness has, indeed, changed a great deal in twenty-eight years.

Take the loon. When we first meditated at Cauc Lake, a pair of loons owned the place. We would see them by day, and at night they would yodel far up the lake and their hilarity would echo back and forth. It was usual for a lake to have one pair of loons and no more. Each pair would raise one or two little ones each season, and a new pair of loons would have to find a new lake. The outboard motor changed that. The loon builds its simple nest right at the water's edge—they can swim like fishes, but their legs are weak on land. So just as a hen loon got settled on her two eggs some damned fool would churn by with an outboard motor and wash the nest away. Maine began to have lakes where loons couldn't reproduce, and over many years the loons adjusted to this and learned to live in company. Lakes that could support loons began to have two pairs, and then three.

Our ornithological research on these visitations is not limited to loons. We look at the perky chickadiddle and identify the purring nuthatch. We feed the gorbies. Once we spent the entire afternoon watching two eagles soar. And one morning a couple of years ago we saw a gaggle of nine loons, together, paddle past slowly as if hoping we'd snap their picture. Cauc Lake is hospitable.

Again, we were having a heated argument over the relative merits of the evening and pine grosbeaks, and our binoculars picked up a cordon, or covey, or caravan, or fleet of canoes coming out of The Siss, which is the thoroughfare connecting Round Pond with Cauc Lake. We gave up our scholarly conversation to watch the rhythmic paddling approach, and we soon counted six canoes. Then they were closer, and we saw the paddlers were twelve Boy Scouts, and that two scoutmasters were not paddling. In my canoe, I said to Bill, if you don't paddle you don't ride. By this time the hour had arrived to begin planning on evening sustenance and we had lost sight of the Boy Scouts as they turned into the cove by the dam. They were out of sight, but not out of hearing, and we heard them laughing and shouting as they had a "dip." While Bill and I do have occasional differences about birds and fishing flies and the morality of Thucydides, we have never quarreled about the supper menu. We readily agreed on steaks, French-fried potatoes, a tossed salad, buttermilk biscuits, several sundries, and strawberry shortcake. It was time to warm the buttermilk. The sun was making ready to set, the lake was calm, a loon was crying, and it was time for Chillingford to appear.

Chillingford was a moose of prodigious size who came over from The Siss each twilight to visit us. In July his antlers were in the fuzz, so we never saw him in widespread autumn splendor. He would hang around all night and we would lie abed and hear him muttering. One night he stumbled over our pick-up truck. Each morning he would come and lay his dewlap on the windowsill and watch Bill and me as we washed the dishes. That evening, before Chillingford came out of his swamp, we got a whiff of woodsmoke from the campground over by the dam, and Bill said, "I think the boys have opened a can of beans!" So we spoke about the tremendous experience it is for a bunch of boys to come from the big city into the north Maine woods and live for a few days like the old *coureurs de bois*, coursing the streams and lakes, breathing clean air and seeing the wilderness sights. To roll into a blanket at beddy-bye and listen to the lullaby of the purling stream. Bill said, "I hope Chillingford doesn't wander over and scare the bejeepers out of them."

The next morning, after we had washed the breakfast dishes and Chillingford had gone, we formed our customary academic procession to gain the salmon pool on Cauc Stream, and we found the Boy Scouts still at the campground. We had expected they would have packed up and be gone down the stream by that time, because Chillingford keeps us from early starts. But there they were. Their canoes were drawn up in a row, bottoms up, neat and tidy. (This may be good Boy Scouting, but don't leave a canoe bottom up. And never leave a camp door closed when you aren't around. Bears. The first bear to come along will smash an overturned canoe to see if it has cookies under it, and then he will smash open a camp door just for fun. Leave your canoes right-side-up. This parenthetical note is included in the price of the book.)

So the Boy Scouts were still there, and we greeted them as we approached. And just then a twin-engine float plane came over the mountain, circled, and touched down on the lake. The engines slowed and the plane drifted towards us. Good sized craft. The Boy Scouts boarded, and off they went to their homes in New Jersey—their wilderness a memory, their "roughing it" done for now. Bill and I watched the plane until it was beyond the mountain, and Bill said, "What next?"

That was the year our state legislature reopened the hunting season on moose. For a generation the Maine moose had been a no-no as an endangered species. So some eager hunter came that fall and nailed Chillingford. There was a little piece about him on the sports page of the Bangor paper. It said he dressed out at almost twelve hundred pounds, and may well have been the largest moose in Maine.

A truck came over the road that afternoon to pick up the duffle and canoes the Boy Scouts had left.

3 A One-Sided Approach

Not long ago the Bangor paper printed a picture of a woman milking a cow. The caption said, "The Woes of Milking." As a proud alumnus of the school of hand-operated bossies I gave this picture good attention. I noticed the stern expression of deep misery on the face of the straining woman. She was certainly having a heavy job of it. I could see there the accumulation of many mornings and evenings of frustration. Then I saw that the cow had pretty much the same expression. A sadness prevailed. And then I figured things out. The woman was milking on the wrong side of the cow! The cow was unhappy about this and was "holding back her milk." She wasn't "giving down." This didn't please the woman, and there we were!

I do not know why cows must always be milked from their right side. I don't recall that I ever asked anybody. I was just told, in the beginning, that I should never milk from the left side, and I tried to. Not too many months ago our magazine *Yankee*, over in New Hampshire, got caught up in this. The painting reproduced on the front cover showed a gentleman manipulating his milker from the port side. The next month the editor answered the flood of letters by saying this was an odd cow, and so was the gentleman, and he always strummed her in a southpaw manner. This is a likely story to me, because if the editor knew that much about cows, why didn't he say so in the beginning?

The removal of the family cow from affairs, and along with her the person who milked her for the family welfare has had a lot to do with changes that have accrued. During my fetching up we had a cow, and I learned to drain her at just about fourth grade. So did most families, and so did most boys. Boys not only learned to milk, but they learned the peculiar ways of a cow— how to care for her and what not to do. No boisterous activity in the tie-up, because cows are sensitive to surprise and have a high startle reaction. Step quietly and never make a sudden motion. A cow who gets frightened will "fall off" in her milk. If things aren't congenial she'll tense and "hold back her milk." If she doesn't "give down" willingly, it's a sign something is bothering her. Cows in a herd, known in Maine more often as a flock, settle their pecking order, and the Number Four cow never tries to walk ahead towards the pasture. Every cow goes always to her own stanchion and eats from her own manger—her crib. Any deviation from established routine is to be avoided. The woman in the picture, with all her woes of milking, is getting just what she should. The most famous left-handed cow was that of Calvin Coolidge.

This was back when Coolidge was governor of Massachusetts and intervened in the Boston Police Strike—1919. He sent his telegram to Samuel Gompers: THERE IS NO RIGHT TO STRIKE AGAINST THE PUBLIC SAFETY BY ANYBODY, ANYWHERE, ANY TIME. This caught the approval of the country, and Calvin Coolidge was nominated for the vice presidency on the ticket with Warren Harding. The Boston *Post* persuaded Mr. Coolidge to pose for some photographs back on the old Coolidge farm at Plymouth, Vermont, and the photographer posed him in numerous bucolic settings. Calvin picked up eggs, fed the pigs, hoed some corn, and took the day's mail from the battered RFD box by the

roadside—with, of course, a copy of the Boston *Post* conspicuous. Then he milked a cow. But before the photographer snapped
the shutter he said, "Governor, I wish you'd shift over to the
other side of the cow—there's a better light."

Pickle-puss Calvin was obliged to smile at this suggestion, and
patronizingly explained that no cow is ever milked from the left
side. The photographer said he didn't know that. "But," he
added, "there's no problem. I do get a better light over here,
and I can reverse the negative in the darkroom and put you on
the right side."

Mr. Coolidge, feeling awkward about it, did pose on the left
side, and the cow was presumably obliging and made no great
objection.

This is not always the case. Cows approached in sinister fashion will usually lift the head with inquisitive expression, look aft
to see what's going on, and then kick the milkpail over into
Somerset County.

The photographer did reverse the negative of Governor Coolidge milking his cow from the left side, and when the print
came to the editor's desk the future president was dexter and
decent, and had what can be considered an amused expression
for him. But the editor noticed that a bag of grain in the corner
of the picture had the lettering hind-side to, and he supposed
the photographer had made a mistake and put his negative in
the enlarging camera upside down. No problem. The editor
merely told the engraver to reverse his negative when he etched
his plate. Accordingly, Mr. Coolidge appeared on the front page
of the *Post*, which was then printing about 800,000 copies daily,
milking his cow from the sinister side. But the bag of grain in
the corner had the letters correct—Grandin Milling Co., Buffalo,
N.Y.

The friendly family cow went her way, and changed so many
things, because of numerous attacks—each as improbable as
another. Not too many, but some, moved along because fastid-
ious people disliked the aroma of a good manure pile that was
illuminating the neighborhood. Livestock got zoned out. But most

important was the gradual intrusion of the Big Milk Trust, which began with pasteurization. Milk produced in Essex Junction, Vermont, had to stay sweet until set on somebody's porch in Newton, Massachusetts. Milk down on the farm, produced by little right-handed Bossie, would sour in that time, but on the farm that didn't matter. Sour milk was used in cooking, or had been skimmed off for butter already, and what wasn't used at the house went into the hogs' barrel and got converted. The milk barons did not, however, condition the public with the contention that it was a long haul from northern Vermont to suburban Boston. Instead, they went after the health angle. Pasteurized milk was good for you. The impression was advanced that it would cure everything. Pasteurized milk had no germs. This abuse of the truth became accepted, and even learned men who should have known better helped promote pasteurization as a bulwark against typhoid fever, gout, soft gums, and dandruff. Also, that was the beginning of the era when housewives were accepting the "just as good" and substitutes and imitations began to abound.

It was about the same time that a big fear arose over bovine tuberculosis. Our Maine legislature approved a policy of "test and slaughter," under which state experts came to a barn, gave the cow a test, and if she showed positive she was hurried to the butcher. The farmer got paid for her by the going price per pound. Later, what was called Bang's Disease or "contagious abortion" became cause for another witch hunt, and after that the state inspectors began coming every Tuesday and Friday, and among everything else looked to see if you put the milkstool on its peg on the wall or left it handy where you could shove it around with one foot. The family cow was helped along to oblivion by the ever-increasing harassment of government inspectors—many of whom were surly and abusive. Many, many, folks said the hell with it and stopped keeping a cow or two. Those with down-east obstinacy who persisted next got visitations from veterinary doctors who were checking things out for the inspectors, and such visitations were followed by bills rendered. The poor little cow, who had been happy, content, and placid, had turned out to be a blamed nuisance. It has been hard, since about that time, to find a proper glass of good, cold milk, or to locate a pound of decent butter.

The day when milk had lumps in it had passed—bilaterally.

4 Lady Law at Odd Moments

Since changing times have overloaded our pathetic courts it has become fashionable to think up solutions. Our good governor recently had a brilliant idea, whatever it was, and probably things will work out. My suggestion, probably as good as any, is to go back to the philosophies that prevailed when crime was so seldom that Judge Larrabee had to make his living from auctioneering. ". . . and many other articles too numerous to mention; the accumulation of a lifetime!" the posters would say, and the auctions always came on a Saturday so everybody could come. Antique dealers hadn't found us, then. There was a pang to those old country auctions of Judge Larrabee's time, for each meant the last fling of a family. The old folks were gone, the children didn't want the place, and everything went up for sale to the highest bidder. After the household goods, the farm implements, and the livestock were sold, the judge would ask for a bid on the land and buildings. A family homestead had ceased to be.

Judge Larrabee was a good-enough lawyer, and served well as trial justice. In Maine we never had the justice of the peace system—a justice of the peace didn't amount to much. He could take jurats, marry people, and if a rebellion broke out he had authority to quell it. Jurats paid twenty-five cents apiece, a marriage fetched whatever the bridegroom thought it was worth, and there is no record that Maine ever had a riot that needed quelling. Deeds and wills helped, but when Blackstone said that "Lady Law brooketh no bedfellow," he wasn't thinking of a law practice in down-east Maine in Judge Larrabee's time. Lawyer Larrabee served as "trial justice," rather than a J.P. He also sold insurance, dabbled in real estate, appraised for the bank, brokered pulpwood and handled woodlots, tutored on the cornet, and played for dances in Rollie Dunbar's orchestra. There was never a time Judge Larrabee's court docket became so crowded he couldn't keep up.

When occasion called, Judge Larrabee's law office over the barber shop became his courtroom. The only difference was the flag. The law said a courtroom must display the United States flag, so when court was about to convene Judge Larrabee would take his flag from his desk drawer and put it on his desk. The flag was three inches by five inches, and he would stick the thing in the mustard jar where he put his lead pencils and his letter opener. Most of the time the complaining officer would be a railroad detective who had caught a tramp riding a freight train on the Maine Central Railroad. The specific crime would be "evading fare," and the punishment was always three months in the Men's Reformatory at South Windham. Most tramps who came to Maine knew that Judge Larrabee was a good fellow, and they were able to contrive to be caught in his jurisdiction—thus gaining three months of comfort during a harsh winter. But if something came up which did not involve a tramp and the railroad, the arresting officer was usually Ruel Hanscom, who was the town constable. Being constable depended mostly on availability and "qualification." Qualification meant that Ruel was bonded. Once bonded, he was qualified to be a police officer, dog officer, truant officer, fire ward, humane officer, sealer of weights and measures, inspector of hay, wood, and lumber, and various other "minor" town officials. Also bail commissioner and court crier. As court crier he would thump his jackknife on a corner of Judge Larrabee's desk and shout, "Court is in session—everybody rise!"

Then everybody would stand up, including Judge Larrabee.

Sometimes, if we had a new schoolteacher who hadn't adjusted yet, she would call upon Ruel to look into a truancy. We boys would be at the swimming hole in Spar Creek and we'd look up to see Ruel on the bank. "Which one of you boys ain't in school?" he'd call, and then he'd turn and go away. In May the Maine water is still too chilly for truancy to be any fun.

So as court crier Ruel was also the assistant who handed items up to Judge Larrabee when he was auctioneering. Always sedate in court, Judge would play the crowds at an auction. If he had too many dishpans and used preserve jars, so that interest began to flag, he'd bring the crowd to attention by whipping up an old-time crockery bed-chamber pot with the cry, "And how much am I offered for this genu-wine Chinese fireless cooker?" With things perked up, he'd return to his dishpans. The judge got a percentage on auction sales, so dangled for every last cent—and usually got it. He kept a supply of chamber mugs on hand to relieve dull moments.

In our town crime ran largely to skipping school for spring swimming, so a big case in the double career of Judge Larrabee and Ruel Hanscom was a cruelty to animals charge against a man who pleaded *nolo* and thus spared everybody the nonsense of a trial. Lady Law, you see, had a slim docket, which was good. Judge Larrabee was never all that great on the bench, but he was the best auctioneer in Maine. There's a moral there, and it probably has something to do with today's crowded courts.

5 Dramatic Improvements

One of our granddaughters was in the regional high school play contest, so you know where I was that evening. She did all right and won some kind of citation, and I was impressed with the giant strides made in classroom dramatics since I trod the boards in my yearning youth. Maybe scholars are better off. The year my ship went down to great applause the taxpayers were still unready to subsidize many cultural advantages now taken for granted, and we didn't have any drama coach. We didn't even have a stage. We didn't have a cafeteria, either, and our English teacher, who also supervised the lunch-bucket noonin' hour, "put on" the annual senior class play. She was good at about anything, and could play mumblypeg at recess so you wouldn't believe it. The town paid her eight hundred dollars a year.

Playacting was not then a letter sport. The senior class play, our only dramatic effort, was not meant to inculcate the histrionic arts, but was supposed to raise money to pay for our graduation photographs. We were twenty-six in our class, the largest in the school's history, and we had to go to Portland on the train to a studio. The round trip cost us fifty-six cents each. Then we had to buy lunch at the Oriental Restaurant before assembling at the photographer's. Afterwards, we had an ice cream at Moustakis's and then caught the evening train home. Big outing, and it took money. So we were strictly a box-office company, and our plays were staged on evenings when the townspeople had nothing else to do.

Miss Ashworth, our English teacher, began by asking how many would like to be in the play. The year before us, only one pupil stuck up a hand, and as monologues didn't draw huge crowds she had to borrow talent from the junior class. But our class turned up thirteen hands, which with parents and friends would promise a good house. Then Miss Ashworth had to find a play that called for thirteen characters. This was no great problem. Plays for high school purposes were supplied by a publisher named Walter Baker, and if you told him how many actors you had, he'd send plays with the right head-count. Except that in Boston there was also a Walter Baker Company that made baking chocolate, and if the postal clerks weren't paying attention there could be a delay. Sometimes it took weeks.

A beautiful stage with an expensive auditorium is available for our granddaughter's efforts, but we poor youngsters had nothing that is today lumped under "equipment." Every boy owned a baseball glove, so we had a baseball team, but nobody owned football uniforms, so we never played football. So we had to rehearse in that portion of the assembly hall that was called the library. The assembly hall was rightly the "main room," and the · library was by the windowsill that had the books. The books were the dictionary and ten volumes of Stoddard's *Lectures.* For those days, that made a rather good library. But we had no stage, so our rehearsals in the library were held up every time a physics class passed to the laboratory. Not having a real stage for practice didn't matter that much, because the Nordica Theatre didn't have a stage anyway.

Named to honor Madame Lillian Norton of Farmington, Maine, who sang under Nordica, our Nordica Theatre was a movie house in the silent days, and what passed as a stage was merely a platform from which the janitor cleaned the screen as occasion required. The "wings" were little alcoves where brooms were stored. But we had no other place to produce our play and we didn't know the difference. Our town never saw a play that had a chariot race, mob scenes, war battles, and anything of size, such as a lawnswing. If something such were essential to the acting, it was simulated offstage. Mrs. Mortimer, who owned the Nordica, ran "pictures" on Tuesdays, Thursdays, and Saturdays, and would rent the place for school plays on an off-day for five dollars. One dress rehearsal was allowed free. The Nordica also had a dance hall. It was to the left of the audience, but open to the theatre, and people could dance rather much in the dark to the music of the piano that accompanied the film. The piano was supposed to keep with the pictures—"The Ride of the Valkyries" for cowboy and Indian scenes, and "Hearts and Flowers" for the love moments—but when the floor was full of dancers the movie viewers got mostly waltzes and fox trots. The night of a play would have neither piano nor dancing.

But there was bowling. Mrs. Mortimer also had a bowling alley beyond the dance hall, with a partition that shut off vision but not sound. It was made with a product known then as "Beaverboard." Bowling went on every night—play, dancing, movies. None of our stage settings could be left in place during a movie, so we had to set up everything the afternoon before the production that night. We could use the movie screen, so we'd hang up things like a woodland or a railroad station, and one year a class used the Parthenon—Hoddie Nutter came to that play to watch his granddaughter, and he thought the Parthenon was Grant's Tomb. Our play, my year, was named *Ruth in a Rush*, and besides thirteen players the cast had a dog.

The dog was lost at sea in a pityful scene of disaster played offstage, but the rest of us made it to shore and came onstage for Act II wet and bedraggled to huddle in misery before the movie screen, which looked like a Pacific atoll with palm trees, serene blue horizon, and fluffy clouds. It is, surely, amazing what we were able to do without taxpayer support, and other marvels of modernity. In my granddaughter's play they had a big thunderstorm with rain beating on a tin roof and lightning and thunder and a high wind. In my day, for our storm, we had a pretty-fair typhoon portrayed back-stage by Nelson Cummings of the school committee and Toodles Bradbury, so-called, who had a dairy farm on the Hardscrabble Road. Nelson blew an oboe and Toodles a tuba.

There was no big contest connected with our play; no competition for citations and a plaque. We wouldn't have won, anyway. The shipwreck scene was the big one. Offstage as we were, dog and all, those with lines had to shout above the oboe and tuba, and also the bowling alley.

The town league was holding the annual championship roll-off that night, and the race was down to the wire. The Knights of Pythias team was trying to overtake the Shoe Shop Shippers, and it was up to Benny Stilkey in the last box. Benny had to strike out.

That was just as our ship went down, giving up the desperate struggle against typhoon and monsoon. Lloyd Towle, our hero, roared out his line:

"WE ARE LOST! ALL IS LOST!"

Benny Stilkey got the strike.

The tumultuous cheer from the Knights of Pythias was not really suited to the tragedy of our dramatic moment.

Do you suppose my lovely granddaughter, with all her school-day advantages, will remember in years to come her high school playacting as I remember mine?

6 The Leash Law

Hardly a trip away from the house but I see a dog walking along the road with a string, exercising his master or mistress as the case may be, and Maine hasn't really been the same since the leash law. True, the leash law hasn't worked, and it may be because the legislature didn't trouble to tell the dogs about it. The other day I had just finished setting forty-eight tender celery plants in a neat row on my tillage when a large, yellow Thomas Cat hastened in a southerly direction and placed a foot precisely on each celery plant as he passed. At once I saw the reason for this unkind intrusion—four large and excited hounds in full cry and unleashed had forced this alacrity on poor puss, and he was eager to gain the sanctuary of yonder limb. The dogs stepped on the celery, too, and then bayed at the treed cat for a while. They left afterwards, probably to hunt for another cat. I regrouped my celery planting and meditated on the leash law.

Dogs that are sometimes restrained seem to revert to natural tendencies when they are not, and go about their business just as they did before the legislature acted. Our Maine legislatures have always been proficient in things the members do not know. I have said many times and am on record that nobody should keep a dog unless he has at least ten acres of open country to deed to the pooch, and that sadness is any dog kept in an apartment. When we had dogs that owned our acres there was much gentility in their manners. I never owned a dog that chased a cat. Farm cats know how to jump on a dog, stick in their pins, and ride him up to the four-corners.

Maine dogs were formerly licensed to "run at large." The expression comes from seafaring. A vessel was sailing at large if she had a good chance-along and the helmsman could relax without anticipation of trouble. This seemed to be suited to the manner of dogs, and was enacted by old-timers who knew what a dog was. The small fees paid to license dogs were not meant to raise revenues, but were intended to make a fund to pay for damage done by dogs as a whole. If dogs killed a sheep, the farmer got a check from the Department of Agriculture, which handled the fund. Also, if a hawk or owl killed some poultry, the dog fund covered the damage. This was a good thing for dogs to do, and they appreciated the chance. Then society got complicated, and agitation began to do something about the dogs running about. The old-time dogs that were too busy taking care of the property were now a nuisance.

We had one good little dog that was half collie and half conjecture that protected our domain while our lad was growing up. This dog, name of Prince, didn't have a collar, let alone a leash, and in utter freedom he attended to every responsibility with diligence. Prince did everything except pay the taxes. He liked to plow. As the tractor moved back and forth across the land, turning the stile, Prince would walk along behind, just abaft the rolling sward. Back and forth, back and forth, Prince would plow all day. And as our lad came along, Prince helped him plow. But by now there was some age on Prince, and the lad had to keep an eye on him, lest he stumble under a wheel. At the end of a furrow, about to turn and come back, the lad was careful not to involve poor, doddering old Prince, who might forget to reverse. So then our lad was grown up, and he went away to do his three years in the army. The next spring he got some leave to come home, and he arrived in apple-blossom time. I had the plow scoured and ready to go. The next morning the lad was up and plowed for two hours before breakfast. Without Prince; Prince had departed this world.

At breakfast, he said, "We need a dog!"

"Second nature," he said. "I plowed so many times with Prince in the way that now I keep looking for him when he isn't there! If I'm going to plow, I need a dog to look out for."

There's reason in that, and poignancy. We got another dog. We named this one Gelert, and he was the one that wouldn't come in the house. We couldn't beg him in. He had a fur coat and didn't mind winter. We fed him on the back steps and he'd bed down in the rhubarb. When the rhubarb waned and winter set in, Gelert still slept there, and if a blizzard covered him with two feet of snow he would bound forth in the morning all eager for his day's work. I told a nice little lady one time that I had a dog that never came in the house and she chided me for abusing the poor thing. We had Gelert and Gelert had us for nineteen years, and he supervised every aspect of operating the farm. He never had a leash. And he never stepped on celery, which may be how-come he lived nineteen years.

Sheemo, who followed, likewise never knew a leash. He liked to wait by the mailbox for the school bus to arrive, and coming and going he barked the youngsters amazingly. We never could get him to stop barking at the friendly school bus. It wasn't just a proper dog's alert—he put on a real whoop-tee-doo. He'd prance and run in circles, and bark until people over on the next road thought he had his tail caught in the door. But once he got the youngsters off to school, reason returned and he wouldn't bark at anything. He'd find a tramp walking up the road and Sheemo would run and meet him and bring him right into the parlor and upstairs, tail wagging and friendly as all-get-out.

So you see I have had ample experience with dogs, and I can see that putting them on a string hampers their style. Today's dogs, roped in, have altogether too little to do, and fettering them is unkind.

7 Vacationland Stuff

The new schedule of television commercials, along with returning geese and the first run of smelts, is ready to attract summer business along in the reluctant spring, and Maine awaits the usual influx of summer complaints, summercaters, seasonal visitors, non-resident taxpayers, and the overnight dogfish. Maine had vacation wilderness camps fairly soon after the Civil War, where "sports" could hunt and fish, but the big push for the tourist trade began in the middle 1920s with Governor Ralph O. Brewster. He proposed our "Maine Publicity Bureau" and after it went to work we soon had the dedicated highway funds from a gasoline tax, our oligarchy of highway commissioners, and soon our first motel. Before motels, all we had was the hotel, and wayside homes with a sign out, "Tourists Accommodated Overnight, $2 a Couple." Whether or not Maine is better off today is much moot-moot, but we are looking for federal funds to restore the charm of Casco Bay, and it's harder and harder every May to find a trout.

By the time our legislature set up a new department called the Maine Development Commission, we were scavenging tourists in a big way and we had several gifted hucksters in the state house who would take their feet down from their desks now and then and come up with "publicity stunts" meant to promote Maine's recreational and scenic advantages. Such wild-eyed schemes were looked upon as news events, and success was measured by the amount of free advertising in the newspapers. There was small radio and less television then, but motion picture theatres did run either Fox Movietone or Pathé news reels just before the "coming attractions." Of the idea-men in our state house at that time, my favorite was Earle Doucette, although the others were nearly as bad. When Earle had thought long enough and took down his feet, something was cooking. Earle had been a newspaperman in Bangor, and his great belief in leisure added class to his agile imagination. He was suited to a state job.

Not too long before the birth of our Maine Publicity Bureau there had been the famous instance of Joe Knowles and his sojourn in the Maine wilderness. Sponsored by the Boston *Post* Joe went naked into the woods to prove that man could survive, like Tarzan of the Apes. His story was not only sound woodsmanship, but top-notch journalism. Joe ran his course, and proved that anything out of the Maine wildlands is a sure thing. Earle proved this to be true several times. One of his first flings introduced Perry Greene. A few preliminary short items were planted in Maine newspapers, and Perry had his reputation established as a competent Maine Guide, a competent woodsman, and a lumber-chopper to out-do even Paul Bunyan. Perry was, indeed, a guide and woodsman, and was also a big man, wide in the shoulders, and amazingly strong. Earle Doucette, of course, did not appear in any of this build-up, and Perry Greene never mentioned him by name. As winter settled in and the big annual Sportsman's Show at Madison Square Garden was due, Perry Greene made a claim that he was the world's champion with the bucksaw, and he would gladly meet all comers.

The bucksaw has been long superseded as a common tool, but in the time of Perry Green and Earle Doucette it was the favorite weapon of the Maine logging industry. Consisting of a saw blade set in a frame, it was a one-man tool for cutting pulpwood and firewood, and because so many Poles worked in the Maine woods it was often called a "Polock Fiddle." Earle Doucette had taken a bucksaw to a "filer," a man who sharpened lumber camp tools, and had him file the teeth and set them so they would rake great gobs of sawdust with every stroke. No man living could endure using such a saw for any length of time, but for ten or fifteen seconds Perry Greene was strong enough to work it through a log. Nobody else had a saw with such a set and such authority, and only Earle Doucette and Perry Greene knew about this one. Perry appeared at the Madison Square Garden Sportsman's Show and met an enthusiastic competition drummed up by Earle's releases. The whole thing was a gigantic hoax, except that Perry did retain his championship, and he did saw through a log in seven seconds. He was pooped, but he did it. The challengers were from all over. The big Swede from Minnesota, who told reporters, "Ay tank aye ban goin' to win," was really Ross Hinckley from Dennistown, in far-up Somerset County. There was also a German, a Finn, a Frenchman, a Greek, and two Russians—all friends of Earle Doucette and all from Maine. Earle made sure that no reporter got to look at Perry's saw, and between bucksaw contests Earle kept it hanging on the wall in the state house behind his desk. All the New York papers had good stories on Perry's first defense of his title, and both Movietone and Pathé got good pictures. Perry appeared at many fairs and expositions for a long time, and was never close to losing his title, retiring undefeated.

In short, for a few dollars Maine got free advertising not otherwise available. In much the same way Earle set up Charley Miller as the world's champion outdoors cook. Charley did operate a small restaurant in Bangor, and did some guiding. Earle would make all the arrangements, and on a Sunday morning Charley would appear. His first stand was in Central Park in New York City, just before (of course) the Sportsman's Show. A policeman walking his beat came upon this man with a tent set up, making his breakfast over a campfire. A canoe was drawn up, and snowshoes and a Winchester rifle stood against a tree. Full of curiosity, the policeman approached and Charley looked up in surprise at being discovered. Charley offered the policeman a plate of flapjacks with maple syrup, two beautiful fried eggs, a couple of pork chops, and several slices of buttered toast. The policeman, taken aback, accepted the plate, and Charley was pouring coffee when the photographers arrived and got pictures. Monday morning editions are hungry for good stories, and Charley was on the front pages.

Charley did get arrested, but the amused judge was lenient, and when it came to the small fine Earle Doucette was ready. Charley's stunt was good just once, but he could repeat in another city, so he was arrested in Philadelphia, St. Louis, Hartford, Baltimore, and Boston. And he drove around Bangor in a white station wagon that advertised his restaurant. Lettering said, "Charley Miller, World's Champion Outdoors Cook." Many many out-of-staters would come to Charley's restaurant and tell him they'd seen him when he camped out in their home-town park.

Maybe Earle's best stunt was the gangster hunt. Back in the prohibition days the mob pretty much took over New York City, and the police were having a hard time. Editorials were clamoring for something to be done. Earle Doucette took his feet down off his desk.

A week or so later, just at morning rush hour, three gentlemen in Maine woods attire got off the train in Grand Central Terminal and walked to the information kiosk. They had red and black checked shirts, hunting knives on their belts, packsacks, and snowshoes under one arm and a deer rifle under the other. "Pardon me," one of them said to the attendant. "We're strangers in town and would like to go to the nearest police station." Every afternoon paper had pictures of this trio, which had come down from Maine in all goodwill to help the police force clean up the gangsters. The morning papers did the follow-up. Then one editor made a telephone call to Augusta and Earle had to admit that he did, in all honesty, happen to know something about the three boys. Earle afterwards chuckled about the small money it took for train fare and hotel bills, and guides' wages, to pick up about ten million dollars' worth of free publicity for Maine's outdoors.

It's been a long time since any such "stunt" came out of our impoverished state house, but Maine does get a lot of tourists. Some of them, more than a few, come in these elaborate Winnebago vans. Great things. Each has its stock of groceries, its saddle tanks of gasoline, its beds and breakfasts—with a boat on top and an automobile on a tow-bar. They come into Maine and befuddle traffic, and they tarry amongst our scenery and use our geography and while they're here they never spend a cent.

8 About Maine Style Sweet Corn

There isn't a corn shop in the State of Maine today. There may be a few of the buildings still standing, but the Burnham & Morrill Cannery No. 19 that stood by Route 4 in Farmington was just lately removed in favor of progress. The hermetically sealed "canned" food was invented in Maine, first as fish, but Mr. Burnham and Mr. Morrill, early experimenters, knew they had a good thing and they soon offered garden vegetables, too. Their biggest problem was convincing the housewife that she could trust something out of a tin can. Sweet corn caught on, and in 1888 a half million cases were processed. "Maine Style" sweet corn was the only kind of sweet corn, and farmers all over the state began planting to supply the demand that grew and grew over the next three-quarters of a century.

The only "Maine Style" sweet corn packed today is grown far from Maine; our production is for local markets only. One by one, the corn shops closed, and even the great Burnham & Morrill company went out of the sweet corn business. The Maine Style corn was also known as "cream-style," because of its milky consistency when tipped from the opened can. But no milk or cream was used in the processing; the appearance comes from the natural juices of the kernels, which are released when the edible part is cut from the inedible cobs. The juices quickly turn milky as fermentation begins, making it necessary for the corn shops to be close to the growing fields. Over a hundred different corn shops processed Maine Style corn in as many towns, and Burnham & Morrill operated about half of them.

Sweet corn grown in Maine is sweeter. But our seasons are erratic, and quality long since ceased to be important in the American food market. Mid-west corn never had down-Maine flavor, but what with this and what with that, "niblets" became the word. Here and there, to meet a dwindled demand, niblets are converted to "cream-style," and appear in Maine food stores to be born again in "corn chowder." Then, here and there a stubborn Maine Mother will scrape off home-grown kernels and "put up" her own winter's chowder supply. Try out some salt pork scraps in the bottom of a family-size kettle, add onions and potatoes, simmer sufficiently, pour in your cream-style sweet corn, add milk (pre-heated lest it curdle!), and simmer some more. You've got a cold-day lunch you can credit to Maine. If you use mid-west niblets, you do not have something "just-as-good-as."

When the summer began to wane and the corn was "filling out," every corn shop began getting ready. Help was found, the retorts were scoured, arrangements made to pick and transport. Cans were stacked, and "closing machines" wiped and oiled. Men did the field work, women got the corn ready for the cans, children came to "husk." When a boy or girl husked a bushel, it was worth a token from the boss, and the tokens were redeemed at the office at quitting time for two cents apiece. You can find tokens that were never redeemed but kept as souvenirs just about anywhere in Maine. If one of them says "B&M" you've a collector's item. In short, everybody turned to and in two to three weeks the Maine corn crop was reduced to rows upon row of tin cans in warehouses behind each corn shop.

The manager of each corn shop was its watchman. He kept things from freezing, and waited until the buyers arrived. They would come in a group, jolly good fellows from the cities, and the waiting manager knew most of them from before. After affable greetings, they got down to business.

"What've you got for us?" one of them would say, and the manager would strike a pose of meditation. "Well," he'd say, "I suppose I'd have to mention the afternoon of August 29th."

The illusion, delusion, or fantasy that one day's pack might be better than another's was carefully kept alive and well. "It's all corn," was the saying in Maine, but the buyers were looking for quality. None of the thousands of cans out in the warehouse was yet labeled. The manager went out and brought in one that he proudly offered as the best of the season—packed on the afternoon of August 29th. He warmed the corn over a Sterno heater and everybody had a taste. "Now," he'd say, "I suppose I ought to mention the 2nd of September, forenoon."

In this way the buyers sampled the season's pack, and orders were placed. The Great A.&P. buyer would take 5,000 cases of September 2nd, to be sold @ two cans for twenty-eight cents, and S. S. Pierce would take 5,000 cases of the same day, to be sold @ thirty-two cents a can. Thus the warehouse was sold out, and no labels had been attached yet. When labels were lithographed and did arrive at the corn shop, the manager started at the front of the warehouse and worked through to the back—

filling orders as the cans came for S. S. Pierce, A.&P., Grand Union, First National Stores, Helpie-Selfie, You-Name-It, and anybody else with credit rating and printed labels. It's all corn.

In packing any food in tin cans, there happens the occasional "dent," a damaged can. The inspector pushes the dents out of the line and they get put aside for local sales. There isn't a thing the matter with a can of dented corn. So local folks, some of whom had worked in the shop during corn season, would come in and pick up a can of dents for little. One year I got six cases of dents of S. S. Pierce cream-style sweet corn, selling in Boston for thirty-two cents a can, for six cents a can. But without labels. Finest kind.

When highways were improved, and trucks could be used, Burnham & Morrill felt their widespread sweet corn operation could be consolidated. They could cut the kernels from the cobs at Buckfield, Farmington, Carmel, wherever, and rush them in trucks to the retorts in the main plant at Portland. No sense in hauling the useless cobs, and money to be saved. They bought a quantity of forty-quart milk cans. After being filled with corn kernels, a can had its flush-fitting cover whacked tight with a rubber mallet.

The new idea worked out fine. The almost-instant start of fermentation, bringing on the "cream" consistency, needed thought, but the testing kitchen found there was no effect on the canned product. Even on hot August afternoons, the fermentation didn't advance enough to be a problem. But fermentation did start, so that upon arrival at the unloading dock at the Portland factory, each can had an incipient charge of fermentation gas inside the hammered-down cover. This was discovered when the first can was opened by pounding with a rubber mallet. The cover took off with a dynamite blast, sailed into the sky, and came down with a crash on the concrete roadway—out of shape and not to be used again.

Before the second can was pounded open, Burnham & Morrill had added a new man to the unloading crew. His job was to catch the covers before they came down and bent on the concrete. For several seasons, this man was carried on the payroll as "left fielder." Inside the plant, canning corn as fast as possible, the workers heard every explosion as a can was opened. If silence ensued, it was assumed that the left fielder had caught the cover.

But now and then he would miss, and the cover would strike the cement with a resounding clang-bang. When this happened, the entire canning crew would shout, "Error Nine! Error Nine!"

So there are comical things to remember, and there was a penny to be made—but Maine has no corn shops today.

9 A Concrete Example

Fiddlehead ferns are in season along the remote upper miles of the Georges River along in May, a delicious harbinger of the season. The first sprout of the ostrich fern has a curled-up tip suggesting the scroll on a violin, and when steamed lightly, given a dash of butter and a touch of vinegar, it makes a magnificent obbligato to any vernal meal. So on an appropriate morning I take my lunch and pack basket and go fiddleheading for a freezer's supply. This is back country, and as I drive along I see mostly woods and scenery, and not too much human activity. Which is good on a fiddleheadin' May morning.

This time, as I drove along, I came upon some unexpected activity. A house was being set in place. This was one of these two-piece factory models brought on trucks, and it was something altogether new amongst the pre-Victorian farmhouses along that road. A cement foundation must have been poured beforehand, and now all was ready. A crane was moving into position. Men stood ready, trucks were handy, and a bulldozer stood poised. I went onto the shoulder of the road and was able to pass, so I kept on going and I had my happy day with fiddle-heads, sumptuous picnic at noon. I can handle not quite fifty pounds of fiddleheads in my "kennebecker" pack basket, and about two-thirty that afternoon I shouldered my load and started for home. It's maybe a mile from the Georges River through the woods out to my parked pick-up at the road. And I came along to the place where the new house was about to be moved into place, and there it was—all ready to be lived in. The machinery was gone; the men had left. The window boxes had geraniums in them. The sod had been laid, and a woman had a hose and was watering the grass. Is it not wonderful what man can do today?

A concrete example of the way things were in earlier times, at least in my earlier times, would be our town's first cement side-walk—the first such municipal improvement in Maine as far as I know. Portland had some brick sidewalks, and I think Bangor had a few places with Monson slate—but slate proved to be slip-pery at times and after a few broken elbows Bangor waited for a better idea. Our town was small, so we weren't supposed to be in the forefront when it came to new ideas. I can remember my first airplane; children today have flown before the age of mem-ory. I can remember when cement was mixed in a mortar-box with a hoe, laid into a form with a shovel, and every moment was considered work. I don't remember the building of our fam-ily farmhouse, in 1790, but Grandfather told me about it and it took quite a while. The house started as a dream when word came that a sawmill would be built at the falls on Little River. By the time it was built, my great-grandfather had logs piled by the place, ready to be the first to become boards. Then the lum-ber had to season a couple of summers, and all the heavy tim-bers were mortised and jointed on wooden horses, made ready to be lifted into place. Great-grandfather didn't have any trucks and cranes and a crew of men—but he had himself, a yoke of oxen, and an able wife to boost and fetch. The family moved into the new home—the first frame dwelling in the township—

in 1800. True, it wasn't an efficient modular home, and it lacked many comforts. But it was a good deal bigger, and it didn't cost so much.

Until the invention of the one-bag mechanical cement mixer, our town had footpaths rather than sidewalks. And just in the village section. Nobody used the paths much, but we walked in the road. It was considered extremely impolite if a man allowed his horse to run over a friend. Maybe the ladies used the paths, I never noticed. But then automobiles appeared, and our main street was paved by the state and became part of Route 1. And then Ike Skillin bought a cement mixer. Just about everybody in town came to watch Ike put a cellarway onto the back of his house, and it was incredible. The thing had a hopper that was turned by a make-and-break gasoline engine; when the mixture was ready Ike pulled on a lever and the thing dumped right into the form. Quite a few people with jobs to be done got Ike to come and do them, and when he wasn't using the mixer he'd rent it out for five cents a bag. Our town moved into a new era. Whenever we heard Ike's en-gyne go pop-pop-skip-pop, we knew somebody was embracing the age of cement and a brickmason, somewhere, was facing oblivion. The mixer was still new enough so people went to watch it, and about that time Ike began promoting a sidewalk. The first stretch, he suggested, should be from the village "corner" up along as far as the Baptist Church, and after that the town could add on every year. Now that he had all the Baptists, our largest persuasion, on his side the project seemed assured.

That first stretch paid for itself in community entertainment alone. After frost-out, Ike began piling clean cement gravel along the route, and he had a car of cement set off on the siding, to be stored in his barn. The route was properly graded, and then the forms for the first thirty or forty feet put in place. As the job progressed, the forms would be picked up and moved ahead. The morning the job started just about the whole town was standing by to watch. Two men shoveled gravel into the mixer, another added a bag of cement and water, and when Ike pulled the lever the form began to fill. The en-gyne popped and skipped, as it was made to do, and as the summer wore on folks could tell from the direction just how far Ike had gained. The wet cement was spread in the form with a hoe, and after elapsed time would be screeded and left to dry. After quitting time for the mixer, Perley Foster would come to stand around and keep cats and dogs, and boys, from making foot marks. Perley was the night watchman, and as soon as the cement had hardened beyond vandalism he would hang on his watchman's clock and go on his route. Today, the town has several police cruisers, real policemen, and at great expense does just what Perley did then.

Along in August the appropriation ran out, but the sidewalk had been built as far as the Baptist Church. Some called the new sidewalk the Baptist Glory Trail, but that never caught on. The next year the town did raise more money, and if we didn't have the first cement sidewalks, at least our town had the first continuing sidewalk program. Also the first sidewalk problems. The boys found the cement great for bicycles, and ladies began to complain about being sideswiped as they walked to the village. The selectmen put up posters and had announcements read in the schools, and this helped. Wheelbarrows, also, were troublesome. A gentleman going to the feed store for a bag of dairy mash found his wheelbarrow almost coasted along on the sidewalk by itself, whereas out in the street he had to push it. When he got rolling right along and came upon some ladies strolling, things did get tacky. So a notice was put up in the post office that ladies, not wheelbarrows, had the right of way. Meantime, Grampie Gilman sharpened his hoe.

It was on a Sunday morning, and Grampie thought it was time to start his first row of green peas. He picked his garden hoe off the barn wall, and decided it needed a touching up. It was, as the saying went, dull as a hoe. A few turns of the grindstone would help, but Grampie suddenly had a better idea. He started along the cement sidewalk, dragging the dull hoe behind him, and he was correct—the cement sidewalk was just as good as a grindstone. It didn't occur to Grampie that he passed the

Baptist Church just as the Rev. Goodrich was reaching the thirdly of his sermon. A morning that was good for planting peas was also warm enough to leave the vestry doors open. The Baptists had their devotions interrupted by the passage of Grampie Gilman, whose hoe delivered an unholy, skin-twitchin', blood-curdlin' screech as it passed, and then repassed. Grampie had to go back home. The next morning in the post office Grampie Gilman had his ears pinned back by a few rip-snorting opinions delivered in his rich pulpit voice by the Rev. Goodrich, who had not been amused.

But a small, unimportant, quiet Maine town had tasted the future.

10 A Little About Mrs. Monroe

A stuffer comes with my monthly bank statement, and my friendly banker tells me the day is not far off when I won't go to his bank at all. This is the latest effort in the planned policy of keeping banks and people apart. When I first had a bank account, saving the first pennies that would see me through college—if I ever survived high school—our banker was Gimlet-Eye Coolidge, and he did everything he could to bring people into his bank and do business. That his right eye gave off into left field was a cosmetic fault, but when his total physique was examined it was not altogether unbecoming. He was built like a Hubbard squash, with spindly bow legs, had a shiny bald dome, and he affected burnsides that came about halfway down and petered out. He wore pinch-nose spectacles on a black ribbon, but they dangled for décor and he never fitted them to his beak when he squinted at a dollar bill. He kept the best horse in town and the high check rein suited the patent leather buggy seat and the real rubber tires on the wheels. He had a ribbon on the snapper of his whip. You could tell Gimlet-Eye was a banker. He knew everybody in town by his first name. Nobody called him Gimlet-Eye to his face; he was respected as Mr. Coolidge. It was his custom to spend the forenoons in his counting house, and then ride out through the countryside on a pleasant afternoon to look things over. He'd rein his horse into a dooryard and say, "Mornin', Thad—great air!" Then he'd say, "Your shed could use some shingles—whyn't-cha come in and I'll let you have the money for a new roof?"

Thus Gimlet-Eye put the bank's money to good use, made a penny as well as friends, and improved the community. He was a benefactor. Today, there isn't a soul in Knox County who knows a bank president from a hole in the ground, and I've just had this letter from mine telling me not to come in and bother him. I'm to get an InstaCard, and with it I can do my banking at the filling station, the barber shop, and the grocery store. No need for a bank at all, really.

Since Mrs. Monroe retired, I've been using a bank in another town, and I mail my deposits and they send back a receipt. Saves mileage. But before that, I did my financial business with Mrs. Monroe. I don't know if Mrs. Monroe's bank had a president or not. She may not have known, either. She kept the drive-up window at a branch bank which had merged several times before it was bought by a consortium and then absorbed by an international conglomerate. The closest I could get to my bank was to stop by and let Mrs. Monroe speak to me through her microphone. I think Mrs. Monroe was the only person that ever worked for that bank who could count over ten without taking off a shoe. She had a regal quality as she sat behind the bullet-proof glass with the little sign that said, "NOTICE—All holdups will be photographed by TV." This was my only brush with new-day banking that related in any way to my boyhood recollections of

Gimlet-Eye Coolidge. She was the nearest to personalized banking since his day. Mrs. Monroe would smile, comment on the weather, correct my addition, and give me a receipt. We had a fiscal, if institutional, romance; she created the illusion that a bank has a heart. But she retired, and on my next visit I found she had been replaced by a somebody who had a "Ms." in front of her name and told me to have a good day. But she told me that only once. I opted for the post office, and I haven't seen Mrs. Monroe since. One day Mrs. Monroe said she thought only two banks in Maine were still owned within the state. One was in Damariscotta, and she thought the other one might be in Skowjhegan. And now comes InstaCard.

Along with my InstaCard, my banker tells me I will get a PIN. This, he says, is a Personal Identification Number, so I can do business with the boy who inflates my tires, the girl who checks out my groceries, and my barber. Nobody will ever know my PIN, he says. It's a secret between him and me. I remember Franklin Delano Roosevelt promised us long ago that nobody except Uncle Sam would ever know our Social Security numbers. But just last week I had to show my SS number to the girl in the paint store before she'd sell me a pint of flat black enamel.

By the way, did you ever hear how we folks in Maine came to have numbers on our automobile drivers' licenses? We didn't have, and of course there's no reason in God's world for a driver's license to be numbered. But other states used numbers, and the automobile rental people began asking for a number when somebody picked up a car. The gentleman from Maine, however, would fly from Bangor into Chicago, and before he could rent a car he had to have a number. So some idiot in our state house decided to be kind to Avis, and the next year we all had numbers. Mine is 3525043, and I never rented an automobile in my life. Such things, one by one, help show what happened to the good old days in Maine.

I shall resist the InstaCard and the PIN as long as I can. It's a losing cause, but there is principle. Another thing about Gimlet-Eye Coolidge—he had a pool table in the basement of his bank.

It was customary for businessmen who came in to do their banking to go below and run off a few points with Gimlet-Eye. The man had been known to foreclose on poor widows, but whenever he made a good shot his merry laugh would rise into the room above, and customers who heard Gimlet-Eye chortle knew that all was well.

11 They Ran out of Wampum

W hen our Maine Indians got their belated land settlement from the timberland people, the Passamaquoddy Tribe put some of its money into a radio station at Rockland. Shortly, after a time with paleface junk music, the Indians turned their FM side to classical music, and all at once the astonished folks of mid-coast Maine were bathed in Brahms, Beethoven, and Bach and we blessed the beloved Indians. It was great; twenty-four hours a day we could enjoy excellent good music. Knowing full well such culture is hard to sustain in today's business world, we prayed that our foolish merchants would do some advertising, and keep the Indians solvent. Our merchants, however, preferred the bang-bang-bang of whatever it is they call "country music," and shortly the Indians shifted back to bang-bang-bang, and that was that. During the lovely meantime, I chanced to say to somebody or other that I had quite a bit of Brahms on some ancient phonograph records, and now and then we'd listen to my record player.

Whoever it was, he said, "Oh, forty-eights, eh?" and I had to explain that I was talking about the granddaddy device—an Edison cylinder that plays just two minutes and I have to wind it with a crank. Offhand, I don't know their speed, but I think it's around 140. Two minutes at any speed isn't much time for Brahms, so the middle of every tune was skipped back in the 1890s when Thomas A. Edison was pioneering the age of sound. Victor Herbert's orchestra recorded Brahms for Edison, and in 1904 Herbert gave up conducting and devoted his time to composing. Give or take, that was a long, long time before today's music lovers embraced the bang-bang-bang. Anyway, a few doubters came to hear my Brahms, and the Edison phonograph proved to be so old hat that it was hard to believe even when playing.

I'm not a "buff," and have these old cylinder records mostly by chance. I never bought any, and some I've always had. People who had them long untouched in attics have given them to me. Friends now and then found some in antique shops and bought them to give to me. Over the years I've picked up maybe a thousand records, and I have six players in working shape. The records that I don't have—records I wish I might have— were in my boyhood recollections and were lost in 1919. My grandfather, who couldn't carry a tune in a handbasket, discovered the Edison phonograph one day and became a lover of good music—and Uncle Josh.

Ours, in Grampie's time, was a remote and uncultured family. Great-grandfather Jacob had come from tidewater to whittle a farm from the upland forest, and finished his big frame house in the summer of 1799. He, wife, and three children moved in from the pioneer log cabin before snow flew, and from then on our family enjoyed comforts. But there still was not heard the sound of cornet, flute, harp, sackbut, psaltery, or any other kind of music, and there wouldn't be until my grandfather discovered Edison one hundred years later. The possible exception would be Lizzie, a state child who had a harelip and could whistle hymns through her teeth. She flourished during the Civil War. Grandfather's introduction to good music was accidental— somehow a rock got into his corn sheller and he needed a new corn sheller. This was a device with a crank, and as one hand turned the crank another fed ears of dry corn into the hopper. Grandfather would crank out a couple of pecks of shelled corn each afternoon for the pigs.

So he went to an auction over at West Bowdoin to see if a corn sheller might be available, and as he was looking over the inventory he came upon some children on the piazza playing an Edison phonograph. He didn't know any such a thing existed. While the auctioneer droned on with the crowd, Grandfather stood on the piazza and listened to "Don't Go Up in That Big Balloon, Daddy," "Corn Huskers' Hornpipe," and—what do you think?— Brahms! Grandfather didn't know anything about Brahms, but the voice on the record came right out, clear as a bell, and said, "Brahms!" I never knew if Grandfather found a corn sheller that day, but he brought home the phonograph and two bushels of records, and this introduction of culture into his bucolic life cost him $1.75. Ada Jones was always a favorite of his, as she was of millions of others, and his collection included three songs—"I'm in Love with the Slide Trombone," "John Took Me Round to See His Mother," and "Just a Little Rocking Chair and You." Ada Jones was a chanteuse of quality and wallop, and had retired from singing by the time a microphone appeared. She did see one—she lived into the 1920s. The way she made records for Edison was a lot like singing into a dishpan. But the quality of the Edison recordings was good—when played on an Edison phonograph in good condition they are amazingly true considering that no electricity was used. Along with Brahms and Ada Jones, Grandfather's repertoire included some Uncle Josh. Uncle Josh was Cal Stewart, who specialized in country bumpkin monologues—Uncle Josh on a Fifth Avenue Bus, Uncle Josh at the Opera, Uncle Josh Goes to a Baseball Game.

Tragedy struck Grandfather's phonograph on a hot July night. Nobody knows how the fire started. A boy walking his girl home pounded under the bedroom window, and Gramp jumped from bed surrounded by flame. Old soldiers don't lose their calm, and Grandfather was an old soldier. He grabbed the featherbed on which he slept and hove it out the window. This was a tick of passenger pigeon feathers that his father had plucked when those birds came by millions and destroyed crops. Long extinct, the bird kept Grandfather comfy and warm, and his first impulse was to save the featherbed. Then he ran into the next room and got his metal box of papers and money. He tossed the box out onto the featherbed, and with the tail of his nightshirt about to burst into flame he poised to leap. There, at his elbow on its stand, was his Edison phonograph, plaintively silent in the glow of the mounting blaze. He grabbed the machine, threw it down onto the featherbed, added the two baskets of records, and then he jumped. The featherbed dulled his thud, but the metal box hurt. He smashed the records and collapsed the phonograph. Otherwise, there was a total loss.

Salvaged from the metal box, the deed to his farm is now in special collections at the Bowdoin College library—the deed was signed by Governor James Bowdoin. He also retrieved his army promotion and discharge—his was Company I, 16th Maine Volunteers, blooded at Fredericksburg, valiant at Gettysburg, traveled in the Wilderness, and from youngster off the farm he had been promoted to First Sergeant. The passenger pigeon featherbed was unharmed, and he slept on it until he died. But the Edison phonograph—alas! I have been able to duplicate most of those records—not only his Brahms but his Uncle Joshes. I can play them for you, and at the drop of a hat I will.

Grandfather and the boy, and the girl, stood there and watched the old farmhouse until it was no more than glowing embers in the cellar. I remember the phonograph on its little table, ready to be cranked. Beside it was a stereoscope with its picture cards. You see, lacking radio, we had the phonograph, and lacking television, we had the stereoscope. We could look at Niagara Falls in Winter, The Palisades on the Hudson, The Vatican at Rome, and even Okefenokee Swamp. Then we could crank the Edison and listen to Ada Jones, Brahms, and Uncle Josh.

Television, so promising, has degenerated into football and sitcoms, and the Indians couldn't make Brahms pay. It is good to reflect that my grandfather did have a touch of culture to brighten his life.

12 The Price of Indifference

The first I heard of this kind of stuff was from Ohio. It seemed, at the time, incredible. The state built one of the first throughways when the big truck era began, and as it was laid out it bisected a certain farm. This was a successful farm, and for over a hundred years it had been raising pigs. Pigs are to eat, and somebody has to grow them. In the high-handed manner of throughway engineers, this farmer was left with half his land on one side and half his land on the other, with some tunnels here and there so he could make do. He was an early victim of non-access. Of course he objected, but he was shushed by eminent domain and the public good. He adjusted as best he could and stayed in business by crossing through his tunnels—but there is more:

Having completed the highway, the engineers in the Ohio state house now laid out a "rest plaza" about halfway of this farm, with tables, fireplaces, toilets, and fenced-off facilities for walking pets. Everything was landscaped to a thing of great beauty. Lovely place. And now they brought action against the farmer because he was growing nasty little pigs too close to the rest plaza. It wasn't decent; it wasn't sanitary; offended the decent folks who paused. He was ordered to stop growing pigs.

So much for Ohio. It was but a few years after that when Maine roused from its happy, down-east, antiquated good nature to embrace the same kind of idiocy. An example is handy. My Dad owned a stand of red oak on the outskirts of peaceful little Free-port village, and one day a man came and made him an offer. The man said he was in the business of building and maintaining wharves in Portland harbor, and he was in constant need of red oak logs. Red oak is used for pilings, and endures under water longer than other woods. The man offered my father $40,000 for the red oak on his lot.

Dad had "managed" this woodlot well for some years, thinking it should help him in his old age, so he was not averse to parting with the trees. But he said he'd insist on having the lot cruised and scaled by a state forester, and only selected trees would be cut. The man agreed to this, said he'd have the "writings" drawn up, and would be back shortly.

But before this deal got any signatures, or money, our Maine State Highway Commission moved in and took most of Dad's red oak woodlot by eminent domain, paying him $250. Dad had walked to the post office that morning to get his mail, and came home with the registered letter about the taking in his hand. Bulldozers had already moved in, and by the time my father got to his woodlot the red oak had been leveled, the logs pushed into a ravine and covered with dirt. And, what is pertinent now, all Dad's good friends and neighbors, who might have rallied to stop this kind of absurdity in the beginning, sat on their duffs with indifference instead of storming the state house to emas-culate the chairman of the highway commission.

Want some more?

Go look at the legislative enactments during Maine's frenzied highway farce—a farce that did more to harm the Pine Tree State than any other foolishness. Find all the bills entered by home-town legislators that asked the state to pay a farmer because his well was ruined. The willing tool of the Maine Good Roads Association, the Maine Truck Owners, the Machinery Cartel, the Insurance brokers, and improbably the Maine Publicity Bureau, our highway commission pursued a planned program of despoiling rural water supplies. Salt to melt snow on the roads did, and does, kill trees, but it also seeped and salted many wells. Ironically, Maine has a good yarn about a salty well. A man who lived in Monhegan Island owned the best well on the island, where good wells are hard to get, and when he decided to sell his place there and live the rest of his life "on the main," he arranged to take up his well and move it. This he did, and had it tied securely to his boat, but some heavy swells halfway to Port Clyde broke the lines and his well went overboard. He salvaged the well all right, and got it to his new home and in place. But it was always salty.

A likely story, but all at once all over Maine country people were complaining about salty wells. The highway commission, naturally, looked the other way with a big fat ignore. The only relief was ask your local legislator to put in a bill and get your value by way of a state appropriation. A casuistry prevailed— highway funds were "dedicated" to highway purposes, and could not be spent on domestic water supplies. Meantime, we were beginning to worry about clean waters and people who sat on their duffs said something ought to be done. Is it not wonderful to consider how well off we'd be today if ? ? ?

Not long ago an interesting lawsuit got some attention in the German newspapers. In a small town not far from Munich called Landsberg, a farmer owned a rooster named Tscheki; the farmer's name was Hans Gebele. Perhaps not everybody is aware that in Germany a rooster does not crow cocky-doodle-doo as he does here in the Boston States, but cries *kikeriki*. True, linguists who have considered this agree that when a German rooster rises tippy-toe on the *Hühnerstange* at *Dämmerung* and lets go with his kikeriki he still sounds a good deal like cocky-doodle-doo, but this is faulty translation. In France roosters incline to the tonic, and say *coquerico*, which is close enough to kikeriki to be almost Teutonic. In classical Latin the dawn cry of the bull chickabiddie was called *galli cantus*, or song of the cock, and the name of the last watch of the night was *gallicinium*. This has nothing whatever to do with a Scottish cockyleeky, so we can now return to our story.

In Landsberg, the rooster Tscheki, belonging to Hans Gebele, was just another scrub rooster until he was brought into court for disturbing the peace—a common nuisance. A reporter on the Landsberg *Blatt* thought a rooster about to become prominent should have a name, hence—Tscheki, which is a nom-de-plumage. A neighbor of Hans Gebele by the name of Rudolf Kofron instigated this absurdity, complaining that when Tscheki went kikeriki at dawn's early light it roused him from the rest to which he is constitutionally entitled, and therefore Tscheki should be rendered null and void. The German judge may well have been versed in American law as regards pigs in Ohio and wells in Maine, because he found for Kofron and remanded Tscheki to the stew-pot. Bauer Gebele has appealed, and Tscheki is out on his personal recognizance. In his appeal, Bauer Gebele has asked the higher court to take notice that Herr Kofron once put up a spite fence and is hard to get along with. He does, indeed, sound like summer people. Bauer Gebele also says, "A person of more or less normal sensitivity will consider the crowing of a cock a thoroughly enjoyable sound." The appeal also suggests, which I find a splendid idea, that Neighbor Kofron would do well to move to the city. I suggest the judge go with him, and also that the neighbors of Farmer Gebele pass the hat and buy two one-way tickets on the *Eisenbahn*.

The little town where my Dad lived, and in which I grew up, had fifteen grade crossings in the village section, on the main line of the Maine Central Railroad, and every night just short of the witchin' hour the Boston-to-Halifax eastbound express would howl through at the sustained speed of eighty miles an hour. The fifteen crossings were within a distance of a mile and a half. If you want to put your slide rule to that, the engineer had to toot his whistle sixty times in a matter of some sixty seconds. Two long and two short at each crossing. This was a rule of the Public Utilities Commission. We were a rootin'-tootin' town.

The Halifax train usually had two sections. The first, making fewer stops, had the all-important mail car, and the sleepers. After it passed, allowing maybe five minutes, the second section would go by with the work cars and the coaches. Nobody in our town ever gave a thought to taking the railroad to court as a nuisance—a kikeriki. We lived with the whistles. We'd get sixty toots, then wait for the second section and get sixty more. But now and then the Halifax train would run in just one section. We'd get sixty toots, and then five minutes later there wouldn't be any second section. This silence would wake up everybody in town, and for the rest of the night we'd fidget in bed.

The chime of the steam-train whistle is not heard in Maine today, and there are those of us who would love to hear it once again. Possibly even Herr Kofron will be sorry when that dreary morning comes and there is no Tscheki to rouse the orient sun and disperse the shadows of night with his amiable kikeriki.

13 Bill Really Wore Spats

The Supreme Court, going along with the lawyers, has agreed to review a libel case. Some newspaper in Ohio had a sports-page story in which a pugilist, or prize fighter, was referred to as a "bum," and the bum decided to take offense. His lawyer was able to make the thing sound important in the writs and allegations, but all it amounts to is the ancient gymnasium dialogue:

Who called my boxer a bum?
Who ever called that bum a boxer?

Which may be amusing, but with a thing like that in court under serious consideration, what's to become of journalism? If honest compliments from hard-working sports writers are actionable, and if every bum with a tin ear can sue for a broken heart, who's gonna-write our athletic news?

The Supreme Court never heard about my Midnight Club. It flourished in the 1930s, and it never got into court because in the 1930s people were—well, people belonged to the 1930s and didn't go to court over nothing at all. I was the new reporter on the local weekly newspaper, and I had to fill the paper every time whether anything happened or not. Bill Murch, Alexis J. Fournier, and I were the original membership of the Midnight Club, but we were joined shortly by just about everybody. Bill Murch was the only man I ever knew who wore spats regularly, and when I suggested it saved on socks he lifted a leg and showed me he wore socks, too. Bill was manager of the town's moving picture house, owned by Boston money, and Alexis J. Fournier was his ticket-taker, usher, and would be the bouncer if a need arose. This was in the tender times of Ann Harding and Jack Holt, and admission at the Cumberland Theatre was twenty-five cents. Except on Thursdays. On Thursday, five acts of vaudeville were added to the "picture show," and the price went up to thirty-five cents.

As ticket-taker, Alexis J. Fournier wore a magnificent majordomo uniform in the finest Hollywood style, braids and glitter, so that going to the movies was much like being welcomed to the palace of some monarchy. Alexis J. Fournier looked a good bit like Jack Dempsey, the prize fighter that was sometimes called a bum, and was accordingly known to the community as Dempsey. Dempsey held down two jobs—when not taking tickets he was assistant chief of police. Sometimes when Dempsey was at the theatre he would be needed for police business, whereat he would give Bill Murch a signal, and Bill would take tickets until Dempsey returned. As assistant chief of police Dempsey had a simple blue uniform that was relatively unimpressive, but when he arrested a tourist on Route 1 for speeding in excess of posted maximum, coming directly from the theatre, Dempsey made quite a sight. Short of a Central American dictator, Dempsey was it. More than a few tourists paid traffic fines meekly and went home to Connecticut to tell about the magnificence of having a summons written by an officer in epaulets.

My duties were comprehensive. I was lucky to have a job in the Great Depression, so I never felt abused. Lots of boys were waving their college diplomas as they joined the WPA and the CCC, and here was I gainfully employed at a welcome pittance. I met all the trains to see who was going and who was coming, I attended all fires, accidents, sporting events, weddings, funerals, birthdays, and after writing the paper I would help wrap the bundles and take them to the post office. I arose before breakfast and lingered late. So it happened one evening that I came along on my walk home and passed the Town Hall just as the big steeple clock was striking midnight. Bill Murch had just dropped his money bag in the bank depository, and Dempsey was standing by as escort. They would part, and each go home his own way. Along I came, and as the clock stopped striking I said, "The hour is at hand—the meeting will come to order!" Thus the Midnight Club was organized.

My first report, in the next week's paper, of the philanthropic activities of the Midnight Club drew no response whatever from readers. Not a peep. After three weeks of the same negative reaction I decided the idea wasn't working, and I didn't write any report. Then I got the reaction. "What happened to the Midnight Club?" "How-come no meeting?" After that, the weekly report on Midnight Club activities continued regularly for ten years—or until I moved along to a more lucrative sinecure.

Membership increased immediately, but most new members knew they'd joined only by reading about it in the paper. After they read that they'd joined, they'd come along at midnight to find out what this was all about—and remain to help with our projects. There was Ralph Buckley, who came home from the merchant marine to operate a sweetshop and soda fountain, and closed his place every night just in time to cross the street and attend. We had an apothecary and a photographer. Allie Despeaux was caretaker at the national guard armory, and he became a regular. Sam Lavallee, night telegrapher at the railroad station, went off duty at midnight and would be about four minutes late. And Steve Ellison.

Steve came from "down south" but had married one of the Gilman girls to become a Maine Yankee. He never lost his Dixie voice. Steve, having married well, had little to do save amuse himself, and he played bridge every night with some cronies in a room in the Town Hall. When the clock struck, he would come forth. Steve was a survivor of the Johnstown Flood, and had a spate of stories that sooner or later turned up in my paper. He told how the police chief at Johnstown asked him to go and sit with a bedridden old lady who was alone in her house surrounded by the rising waters. Steve got himself two quarts of bourbon whiskey, and the police delivered him to the woman's upstairs bedroom in a boat. When Steve took his first draft to prepare himself for the vigil, he noticed the little old lady had a twinkle in her eyes and was trying, feebly, to tell him something. Trying to understand, he gestured to indicate he was offering her his glass, and she nodded. Steve's punch line was, "And would you believe that I made a drunkard out of that fine woman?" At bridge, he was just about unbeatable. I'd seen them deal out four bridge hands, face down, and Steve would pick up the first three, one at a time, look at the thirteen cards, and replace them, still face down, on the table. Then he'd tell you the cards in the fourth hand. So Steve became a member of the Midnight Club, and I think the Gilman family was not altogether amused. At one meeting, Steve moved that we impeach the governor and turn all his executive duties over to the Kora Shrine bagpipe band. The motion was carried. Quite a number of readers wrote letters to the editor, saying this was a splendid idea and they would gladly sign our petition. There was scarcely anything the Midnight Club didn't tackle.

Almost every line of my weekly reports was libelous. Nothing happened, because in those days people were not court-minded. People didn't get mad. Anything in jest was recognized as such. Our readership was amiable and liked to smile. Can you imagine the businessmen of a community, today, standing on the sidewalk at midnight, voting on a proposal to move Mount Katahdin down to Cumberland County? Even if that happened, Maine doesn't have an editor in this age of lawsuits who would print it.

14 Peace and Poverty, Fess

In pondering what the computer age has done to the State of Maine, I've decided it has done just about the same as elsewhere, but that doesn't cheer me up at all. I have a friend who is a lawyer because he flunked out of divinity school, and he came by the other day to borrow my red sneakers to wear to a wedding, and I asked him if an aggrieved citizen has any recourse when he gets caught up in a computer and can't get out. He gave me the following advice, "Ha, ha, ha."

He then told me that he had recently suffered severe anguish and continued emotional distress when, by computer error, he got twenty-three consecutive monthly bills from the gas company for $00.00. After he had ignored the first three, succeeding bills were accompanied by nasty dunning letters impugning his character, and finally he was brought into small claims court. He defended himself in this litigation, and quickly proved that the bills should have gone to quite another person of the same name in Yonkers, New York, where there is a gas company. He said the judge was sympathetic, and awarded him punitive damages of $00.00.

At the time, I was in much the same kind of disrepute over our family coat of arms. This was back quite some time before Christmas, and I have been getting nasty letters ever since that could, I suppose, bring me finally to small claims court. It was a quiet evening with popcorn and my wife was looking at the junk mail. She said, "I didn't know we had a coat of arms!"

"Oh, yes," I said. "It comes down from Attila the Hun on one side, and on the other side it says, 'Made in Taiwan.' "

"It says here," she said, "that we have a coat of arms and that I can get it on a crystal goblet. Doesn't say where it's made."

"Very interesting," I said.

"Wonder what our coat of arms looks like?"

"Why don't you buy a crystal goblet and find out?"

"I don't want a crystal goblet."

Conversational tilts like that are not at all uncommon in our family and after one I always find it difficult to compose myself and return to my contemplations of the theocracy in the reflections of Alcibiades, or whatever, so I stared at the wall a little while and wondered, too, what our coat of arms might look like and why it would be on a goblet. I was much relieved when she said, "I think I'll send and get one."

Life has not been the same here in Maine since then.

The goblet arrived, and it is beautiful. Somebody with talent and a generous imagination cooked up a coat of arms for our family and we are as well fixed as the Plantagenets. Inasmuch as our family came out of midland England in company of coopers, thatchers, poachers, shingle shavers, and assorted low-life (although respectable) tax evaders who were requested to leave by the authorities, the presumption of heraldic escutcheons is whimsical. If we should have a coat of arms coming down from 1066 and all that, it would likely show two pitchforks crossed against a field of winter rye, gules and fess, with the motto, "Peace, Poverty, Penurity, Paucity." If such existed, I can hear my grandfather saying that Peace is a misprint for pease, as in pease porridge hot. So thanks to a glass blower somewhere with a smart merchandising assistant, and my wife's addiction to mail-order come-ons, I now have a valid armorial bearing that I can apply to a bedsheet and ride about redressing human wrongs. With all the dashing derring-do of good Sir Galahad himself.

So having seen what the family coat of arms looks like on a

crystal goblet, my wife sent a check, terminating the armorial quest and closing out the matter. So we were told and so we thought. Since then, every month, we get a box with two more crystal goblets, and coat of arms, and then the bills and nasty letters—each bill with the additional 18 percent. It's like that machine grinding salt down in the ocean. There's nobody to talk to. The goblets come from Georgia, the bills come from Montana, and the nasty letters come from New Jersey. Here in Maine the man at the post office told me, "Well, what you have to do . . ." I cut him off at that, saying, "Look, Mister—I don't HAVE to do anything!" And I don't do anything.

15 Five Times Five Is Twenty-five
(Sing to "Yankee Doodle")

A prudent householder, in the happy times that were, would buy his flour by the barrel. If he lived on a farm, he brought it home in the wagon. If in the village, it was brought into his pantry by the grocer's delivery man. Is it not amazing that grocers used to deliver? The barrel of flour, at least in Maine, was significant in folklore—babies were not brought by the stork, but came in a barrel of flour. In my growing up the only bread we bought at the store was "stale." Mother used stale bread to make the stuffing for a roasted rooster. If we'd just had a supper of French Toast, there'd be no stale bread in the bread jar, so she'd send me to Magoon's Market with six cents to get a loaf of stale bread. "Ask for stale bread," she'd say. Mr. Magoon knew why, and he'd say, "Ah! Roast chicken for Sunday!" He'd take my six cents. Fresh bread was eight cents. Mother believed stale store bread was "better'n nothin'," but she never in her life bought fresh store bread for our table. There is no such thing in a store today as a barrel.

Now, in a new generation, my live-in cook said, "We need bread and I'm all out of flour!" This would have been the first true family catastrophe since Uncle Aaron caught his famous beard in Grandmother Deborah's flaxwheel. Gracious living was at stake. Gracious living, with us, is home-made bread. Expense is no object. I already had my boots on by now, and grabbing my checkbook I headed with alacrity to the Shav'n-Shop Super-Duper Market, where I hefted a twenty-five-pound bag of Robin Hood All-Purpose Flour and returned home. Within due time our house smelled of baking bread, and he who lives in a house that smells of baking bread knoweth not cark nor care and would not swap for the golden bounty of the Garden of the Hesperides or the luxuries of storied Xanadu.

"Give us this day our daily bread" is redundant, and doubly emphasizes my gratitude.

When the bread is properly crusted and she brings it, loaf by loaf, from the oven to advertise itself among the counties, and she anoints it adroitly by stroking with a stick of butter, the resounding aroma has no equal and few rivals, and my heart leaps in joy. A childhood treat was to have a "heel-tap" from a loaf of hot, new bread and run with it to play. Sometimes I—we—had to wheedle, because Mom wasn't eager to slice hot bread. Cuts better when cool. But if we prevailed, she would slather a slice—preferably the heel-tap—with our home-made cow's butter, sprinkle dark brown sugar, and smear with Barbados molasses from the earthenware jug. Nectar and ambrosia were for poor people like Zeus and Hera. In a family with cooperative children a first loaf of a new batch would be thus sacrificed, and that would mean two heel-taps. When we were aroundabout and baking bread announced its flavor, we children at our dooryard pleasures would perk up and sniff. Satisfied that we

71

had read the message aright, we would start for the kitchen pell-mell, and the most alert would already have yelled, "I hosey the heel-tap!"

If it seemed likely enough slices would be cut, somebody else would shout, "I hosey heel-tap number two!" Hoseys were usually respected, but sometimes Mother would say, "No—you've had three hoseys in a row; let your sister have a chance." There was a story in our family about a boy down the road who was "spoiled rotten" and bargained with his mother. Maybe she bargained with him. He'd learned to hold out for his price. My mother prophesied he'd grow up and be a union boss. Anyway, if his mother asked him to do some errand, he'd say, "I will if you give me a cent!" So she'd give him a cent, and it was more her fault than his. The boy became a horrible example in our family, because we were taught to jump if Mother wanted something. One baking day this boy's mother wanted him to do something or other, and he stood a moment thinking what tribute he should demand for being an obliging young man. While he was thinking, she said, "I'll give you the hot heel-tap with brown sugar and molasses!"

Jimmy considered this. "All right," he said. "But mind you put a good bit about the crusts."

Accordingly, we always reminded Mother to put a good bit about the crusts, adding jollity to what was already jolly, and if Mother didn't have molasses on her fingers she'd cuff the nearest one of us on the ear.

So my heart was brimming over with love and fond memories when I brought home that twenty-five-pound bag of Robin Hood flour—the all-purpose flour. She had said Robin Hood flour, so when I came to the shelves I was careful. A boy was there, a minion in the super-market industry, and he was arranging and replenishing the displays. There was Pillsbury's Best, Gold Medal, and King Arthur. "Point at the Robin Hood, Good Will Stutly," I said, and Good Will Stutly pointed at the Robin Hood.

"Prithee, right here," he said. I hefted the twenty-five-pound bag and strode forth as a bridegroom. When I got home, she said, "How-come you got the twenty-five-pound bag?"

"You told me to get twenty-five pounds of Robin Hood flour."

"That's right."

"So I got you twenty-five pounds of Robin Hood flour."

"Yes, but why didn't you get five five-pound bags?"

I burst into song, to the tune of "Yankee Doodle":

> Five times five is twenty-five,
> And six times five is thirty,
> Seven times five is thirty-five,
> And eight times five is forty.

Stupid me. The twenty-five-pound bag cost $4.49, but right beside it on the shelf were the five-pound bags, on sale at 69 cents each. Special, this week only. "How-come you didn't notice that?"

I responded thusly: "How-come Will Stutly didn't tell me?"

So what? Expense is no object. I may be, but hope I'm not, the only lucky fellow in all Maine who still has the chance to hosey a heel-tap.

16 The Day I Played MacHamlet

"The actors are come hither, my lord," said Polonius, and while Hamlet mocked him he was also glad for the news. When will actors come hither again into Maine? We used to have actors come. When Lakewood Theatre was the big thing, we had plenty of players visit us who thought they were well rewarded by a free vacation on lovely Lake Wesserunsett, and in addition to the stage plays we were amused when, for instance, Keenan Wynn was arrested five times in one week at Skowhegan for speeding his motorcycle. He never got that much attention in Hollywood.

One morning in 1932 I was sitting in my secular sanctum at the Brunswick *Record* when a man came in off the street to say, "The actors are come hither, my lord!" Brunswick did have a tinge of culture in those days—the lectures and concerts sponsored by Bowdoin College were always open to the public, and now and then the college dramatic club would try something special. But this gentleman who breezed in had nothing to do with the college—he was the advance man for a barnstorming troupe that played Shakespeare—possibly the last troupe of its kind ever to favor the State of Maine. He affected a Dickensian manner, something W. C. Fields was to do better another time as Mr. Micawber. He told me his company was booked at Portland and at Bangor, and between those communities they would make a one-night appearance at Brunswick. *Hamlet*, he said and he handed me two free tickets meant to encourage me in granting some free advertising. He expected, he said, to be successful in a community like Brunswick with its fine academic institution. He said if I cared to offer any publicity, he'd like to have me say that his company always used local talent if any applied. That appealed to me, and I told him to set me down. It was to be my only appearance on the professional stage, but as it turned out I played a very prominent part.

So for the next few issues of the *Record* I stuck in squibs about the coming of *Hamlet*, and I did say that local people would be used in minor roles. Interest developed about town. Some of the professors at Bowdoin suggested their students attend, and Professor Stanley P. Chase, himself, said he would be there. Professor Chase was chairman of the Department of English, and taught Shakespeare. I remember as I wrote these little advance squibs I thought of the review of *Hamlet* that Bill Nye wrote for his Laramie *Boomerang*. Bill said there was general rejoicing when Hamlet died, but the audience was mad at Laertes because he killed

Hamlet before they could get to do it. Nothing downright as that would appear, you bet, in our sedate weekly! I did my notices straight, lest they make the unskillful laugh.

On the day of the big event, I went to the railroad station to see the players come hither, and was a bit disappointed at their appearance. The actors looked just like other people. There wasn't a Mr. Micawber, a Sir Henry Irving, a John Barrymore in the bunch. Their manager pointed at the Eagle Hotel across the way, and the company walked to it while the manager conferred with the baggage master about the trunks. This company stood ready to do any one of some fifteen Shakespearean plays and had all the costumes and properties in a great number of trunks. Only the *Hamlet* trunks would be needed in Brunswick, and all the others would wait at the depot.

Hamlet did draw a good crowd. The college people turned out, and so did the "townies," and the Town Hall was filled. The old Brunswick Town Hall, since demolished, had a fairly good stage and auditorium, with adequate lighting equipment and reasonable acoustics. At the proper time I appeared and climbed the back stairs, ready to do my walk-on part. I was to be a Thespian! I was halfway up the stairs when the wild shriek of bagpipes assaulted me, and at the top of the stairs stood a braw Highlander in plaidie and kilt, brandishing a claymore that would fell a moose—beside him a piper fondling his doodlesack.

The traveling players were all ready to render the tragedy of *Macbeth*. The house was waiting for the tragedy of *Hamlet*! I ducked under the claymore, found the manager, and he said, "Odsbodkins! I didn't know that!"

He gave quick instructions for the players to adjust, and he streaked to get the *Hamlet* trunks. Everything worked out fine. All the players played all the parts, so to speak. Lady Macbeth was also Gertrude. The First Gravedigger was also the Porter. Osric would be Malcolm. And, the Scottish moors would be the platform at Elsinore. Except that Bernardo, Francisco, Marcellus, and Horatio were still in their kilts. So the first scene, on the platform at Elsinore, was played without lanterns, and the 145 lines were drawn out to forty-five minutes. By that time the *Hamlet* trunks were at hand, and I watched as the bagpiper discarded his kilt and got into the costume that turned him into Guildenstern. And then the witches' moor was lighted to become the throne room with Claudius and Gertrude.

I remember how casually the players handled this mix-up. Nobody got excited; nobody seemed to think anything was amiss. The production of *Hamlet* was so acceptable that even Professor Chase said so.

My part in the play? I was one of the three "rabble" that helped Laertes break down the door when he was hunting for his father. Otherwise, I suppose, I might have been invited to the coronation at Scone. A pleasant memory of the days that were.

17 Let It Simmer Three Hours

The way things change and are never the same covers piccalilli day, too. And this year our house didn't resound as usual to the wild cry of the pickling piccalilli. "Seems time to lay by some piccalilli," I said, but she demurred because she had some jars left over from last year, and some from the year before, and there wasn't shelf room. So we've skipped this year and will still have piccalilli—and that means we've skipped the glad afternoon of afternoons when I step from my bright fallish environment into the kitchen and brace myself against the powerful exuberance of residual piccalilli momentum that slaps me between the eyes and makes me glad. There is no other day so joyous as piccalilli day and no other attar so handsome.

This was not a season to skip. For some reason the gardens around here disliked to bring on the ripe tomatoes. I never did pick one that was vine ripened. Plenty of green ones that turned red on the windowsill; other gardeners told me they had the same reluctance. Some said it was the lack of sunlight in the spring; some said too much rain. Piccalilli is made with green tomatoes. So everybody should have made a lot of piccalilli. The Extension Service, besieged with requests for green tomato recipes, began feeding them to the newspapers. This caused Barbara Whitney, a young and comely friend and neighbor, to telephone to my wife to say, "This here piccalilli reseet in the *Courier* confuses me. You make a good piccalilli—whyn't I use your reseet?"

The dictionary confirms my spelling of piccalilli and says it is a highly seasoned pickle of East Indian origin made of chopped vegetables. Here in Maine it is specifically the Saturday night relish on a plate of hot baked beans. We use it for other things, and it goes well on a hot dog, but baked beans without piccalilli are a pie without apples. My wife told Barbara she has a number of piccalilli recipes, no two alike and all different, and it's hard to find one that isn't good. Barbara said, "Give me the one you use."

What makes the kitchen heavenly on piccalilli day is the lingering commingling of sweetened hot cider vinegar with its charge of mixed pickling spices. The air hangs with it. The vegetables are green tomatoes (1 peck), 4 sweet peppers, and 12 onions, chopped. Some put them through a meat grinder, but others say grinding isn't good. Use a wooden bowl and chopper. My wife told Barbara, "I use my mother's reseet. I've got others from other mothers, and John's mother, and my mother, but I use my mother's."

Barbara said, "What was that you just said?"

My wife added, "And I've got a very good one from the *Mizpah Class Centennial Cookbook.*"

Barbara said, "Let me have the one you use. I'm ready."

Then followed the reading of items and the pauses while Barbara wrote. But two women doing their housework on the telephone make their side trips, and while I listened (I was oiling the clock) I heard the digressions. On one of them, I learned that Paul Wolter finally got the *Economy* to Jacksonville. He and his wife, with our friends Dick and Betty as crew, started south and for some reason missed the entrance of the canal. It was after dark. Then contrary winds persisted. Now Paul had telephoned to say *Economy* was safe on mooring in Jacksonville. This was between the onions and the draining of the mixture. Now drain overnight.

Next morning, she said, add 8 cups of sugar and pour on vinegar to cover.

Barbara said, "I got it!"

My wife said, "Then you simmer for three hours."

"That's when the house begins to smell so good?" Barbara asked.

"No, not yet," said my wife. "Let it simmer for three hours and then you add one ten-cent package of mixed pickling spices. That's when the house revs up."

"Add *what?*" said Barbara.

"A ten-cent package of pickling spices."

"You're outa your mind!" said Barbara.

"I'm reading my mother's own handwriting!"

P.S.—Friendship Market now charges $1.89 for a ten-cent package of mixed pickling spices.

18 Grandmother Was Grateful

The man came and looked, and he said, "No sense in putting a new motor on a washing machine that's already ten years old!" The moral of that is—never ask a man who sells new machines to fix an old one. So I had to say, "All right—bring me a new washer." So he did, and we now have a new washer—and an old one that doesn't work. I told the man, "My grandfather had a washing machine motor seventy-two years old and it ran like a new one!"

He said, "How could that be?"

I said, "You're too young to know about values," and when I wrote him a check he looked at it closely. He doesn't see many checks—he thought I was going to finance the thing.

My grandmother, who was the motor for my grandfather's washing machine, never saw an electric light bulb. Maybe she had seen a flashlight, or an automobile at night, but her farm never had electricity. The washing machine that lightened her laundry day was, to her mind, a big improvement over no machine at all. And this wasn't, really, all that long ago. I can remember the first "binder" that came to that farm to reap the grain. It was drawn by a team of horses and was a sensational innovation. A Scot named Colin MacQuarrie had invested in it and for so much a sheaf was harvesting the oats, barley, and wheat of the township. Everybody marveled that a machine could tie a knot in string! Each sheaf was bound and that's why the machine was called a binder. The combine was still ahead. Colin pronounced it "boinder." The machine could count, too, so instead of tossing off a sheaf at a time, it waited until it had seven sheaves. Seven sheaves made a stook—three to a side and one on the end. The grain dried in the field in stooks and was brought later to the barnyard for threshing. Colin would say, "Daresay some day we'll see a boinder that will e'en stand oop the stooks!"

Such modernism in the field was equalled by the wonderful new washing machine in the house! Grandmother's origin on Skye didn't set Mondays as wash days, so when there was laundry to do she picked a "dryin'" day, whichever it was. The washing machine was trundled into the kitchen from the shed, along with two wooden tubs and the benches on which they fitted. The washing machine was a third tub, and it had a wringer clamped to the side. This—soaking, washing, and rinsing—took up most of the kitchen, and we sprouts knew enough to keep our distance.

Grandmother knew nothing about running water. Every drop of water—for house and barn—was lifted from a dug well by rope and crank. The well house stood halfway between the barn and the home, equally handy to both. Water was carried in pails that everybody called buckets. The menfolks did draw and carry the laundry water, which was heated on the wood-burning range in the kitchen. In a separate and smaller container, the "junk" of home-made hard soap was "loosened" in warm water. When all was ready, right after the usual six o'clock farm breakfast, dirty clothes, hot water, and soap were put in the machine. The home-made "cast iron" soap was now like jelly, and it didn't hang back when it came to things like ring-around-the-collar. The machine had a hinged cover that folded into place, and the four pegs that made it look like a stool were meant to agitate the laundry. They twisted back and forth when Grandmother cranked, which she now did with as much effect as any motor. Later came rinsing (rensin') and wringing, and other loads that followed until wash day was accomplished. Hanging out the wash on the dooryard clothesline wasn't too big a chore except in winter, when things froze before they got pinned up. Grandmother was thankful she had a washing machine.

One time I was giving the grandchildren some of this history, and I got the question, "Why didn't the menfolks come in and turn the crank?" I said, "Women's Lib."

I said, "You don't want to think the emancipation of the ladies is a new-day idea, because it isn't. The men were out plowing and reaping and cutting firewood and feeding the pigs and shearing the sheep and milking the cows, and all sorts of things like that, and they were perfectly happy to have so many things to keep them busy. So it was agreed all around that if the women didn't come out in the field and ram around and butt in, the men would leave them in complete charge of the house."

19 How Long Is a Plutt?

E very so often some nut threatens us with the metric system, so we folks in Maine have been interested to see how the thing worked out in New Brunswick. Just over the border from our city of Calais, the New Brunswick town of St. Stephen has a sign welcoming the visitor to Canada, and then it says,

NOTICE
All Highway Distances and
Speed Limits in New Brunswick
Are Posted in Metrics

Not long after that sign went up, we drove over to a St. Andrew's meeting at St. John, and right under that sign I pulled up where a policeman was standing at the curb.

"Good morrow, kind sir," quoth I, and he leaned over to hear what I might say. I said, "How far is it to a decent motel that sets a good table?"

He smiled. "Welcome to New Brunswick," he said. "Exactly five miles."

Without reference to that, as the New Year approached and I girded (poetically, of course) for the next, I was pleasantly reminded by an advertisement on the radio that I should replace my permanent anti-freeze. The next day I paused at the establishment of my long-time friend. Petruccio O'Brien, which is a filling station, and I asked Petruccio, "Why would anybody need to replace his permanent anti-freeze?"

Petruccio is a good boy, and now he laughed a good, round, hearty laugh that jiggled him all over and caused him to lean against the unleaded pump until he could catch a breath. When recovered, he said, "Trouble with you is that you know too much. They don't teach things in school nowadays that they did back along. Today, nobody knows what permanent means. That commercial on the radio scares people and one day last week I replaced three hundred dollars' worth of permanent anti-freeze with permanent anti-freeze."

"You're a crook," I said.

"That's one word for it, but another is that I'm the happy beneficiary of clever modern advertising and the inefficiencies of a high-priced school system."

"Is there a resale value to recycled permanent anti-freeze?"

"Yes, they is, but I ain't crook enough to go after it. I dump the stuff in a drum and give it to Tooby Ruggles down to Ash Point."

"Tooby?"

"Eyah. Tooby's a plumber and every fall he has to winterize all the summer cottages. Applesass Cove, Ash Point, all the islands. He laces the plumbing with used permanent anti-freeze and it's a lot easier than draining pipes and flush bowls. He sells the stuff to the summercaters for ten smacks a shot. Tooby's a crook."

I told Petruccio about reading in the paper that a superintendent of schools said kids don't go to school now to learn—they go to be entertained. Petruccio said, "Cheers for him! But if kids are ever taught again what words mean, it'll cost me a good many smackeroos a year per annum. I put two kids through college on replaced permanent anti-freeze, and neither one of 'em knows which mitten goes on which hand."

"You jest," I said.

"Some, but not all that much."

With the mitten on the other hand, I still don't know what the Richter Scale is. Every time there's a rumble, the "media" tell me it measured so-and-so on the Richter Scale, and nobody has ever offered to tell me what that is. My dictionary and my encyclopedia are silent, although I find there was one Richter, long ago, who played the piano. A piano scale? I know about oyster-shell scale on fruit trees, and the peculiar nine-note scale of the Scottish bagpipe. The Beaufort Scale measures air movement. But there was a time reporters and editors were careful about such things. Remember when the bandits robbed the Brinks Express in Boston? Not too many people, particularly us bumpkins out in the sticks, ever heard of Brinks Express. So every newspaper properly had a paragraph explaining that Brinks Express transfers money for banks. Very good. In those days newspapers cost five cents.

And I remember one story I did myself about a carpenter who was building a cupola to go on the roof of a barn. Somebody told my editor about this and said it might make a story. I walked two miles in the hot sun out over the Beech Hill Road, carrying a 4 × 5 camera, and found the carpenter at work. He was making the cupola on two wooden horses on the ground, in the shade. He hadn't found it necessary to go onto the roof for measurements—he knew his geometry and the pitch of the roof. Simple pencil work on a board. And I found he didn't use feet and inches—or metrics. He didn't know what he used.

When he started a job he would take a stick and divide it into equal sections with his compasses. Then he'd divide the sections into subsections until he had something like a yardstick except that he didn't know how long the stick was and how long was each section and subsection. "It doesn't make any difference," he told me. So long as he went by his stick, it didn't. When he finished a job he'd toss his measuring stick onto the scrap pile, and make a new stick for the next job. He liked to make up names for his distances, and on this cupola he had invented threetles and quitchets. Four quitchets made a threetle. But when they brought a crane and hoisted the cupola to the roof, it fitted.

My editor, after he read my first paragraph of the cupola story, decided prudence was called for, and he didn't ask me to elucidate about pobbles and plutts. But for the reader's sake, I did make things clear. Two plutts to a pobble, and six pobbles to the seeple. So what is the Richter Scale?

The same day that I had this illuminating conversation with Petruccio O'Brien about permanent anti-freeze, I came home and the flaxen-haired miss across the way stepped in to chat. She is ten jolly years old, and I asked her if she'd ever read *Alice in Wonderland*. "I don't have to," she said. "I've got it on a tape."

20 The Advantage of Junk Mail

How pleasant it was to walk out to the road on a joyous morning and meet Jethro Murdock when he brought the mail! The Rural Free Delivery was established in 1896 as one of many things the United States Government introduced to bring happiness to the farmers. My Grandfather told me how it was before the RFD—anybody going to the village would pick up things at the post office and drop them off on his way home. In turn others did the same. There was no schedule, and if nobody in the neighborhood had an errand at the village a week or more could pass without mail. Then he got a mailbox at the store, cut a hackmatack post, and was ready the first day a mailman came. Every day except Sundays and holidays, after that, the mail came faithfully to his box by the roadside—which from the beginning was numbered 35. RFD 1, Box 35.

When the RFD started, the postmaster general issued regulations about the boxes. Each box had to be "approved," and must be set on the right side of the road as the delivery was made. It had to be set so high, and must be kept clear of snow. That is, the RFD was set up to accommodate a driver riding in a buggy behind a horse—or a sleigh in winter. Buggy drivers sat on the right side. Buggy seats were so high. When automobiles came along, which were driven from the left side, nobody bothered to change the rules about boxes. Postage advanced from one cent to, as of today, twenty-nine cents. And the simplicity of country mail got involved with junk mail. Grandfather used to get his *National Tribune* once a month, and his *New England Homestead* every other week, and his regular Grand Army pension check. Now and then he used to take a subscription to the Lewiston *Evening Journal,* but if that lapsed he didn't always bother to renew. He liked the *Journal* for kindling fires, and he used a page to wad his musket if he had occasion to shoot a fox in the henyard.

Jethro Murdock was the route's first mailman. If anybody was waiting at his box, Jethro would visit a moment in addition to making his delivery. He sold stamps, made out money orders, and was never in any great hurry. In Grampie's time, many a day there would be no mail. When Grampie's pension check came, he would hitch up Old Fan (if 'twere a pleasant day) and drive to town to cash it at the bank. He'd get the few groceries a farmer needed, perhaps have his hair cut and his beard trimmed, and usually took a case of eggs to trade. All the other old soldiers had come to town to cash their pension checks, so there was reminiscence.

After Grampie ceased to need mail service and I took over his box, our mailman was Charley Smith. Charley had a low-slung automobile that came nowhere near buggy height, and he drove on the left side. He had to do a contortionist act to get into our mailbox at all—and it was the same box Grampie had set in 1896! I suggested to Charley one morning that I could easily set the box down on the post so he could reach it without bringing on a chiropractic adjustment, and Charley was aghast at the thought. "Can't do it!" he almost shouted. "Can't do it! Regulations!" The rules of 1896 prevail.

For long years it was cheaper to mail a bundle from an RFD box than to take it to the post office. This didn't make sense at any time, but it came to sheer idiocy in wool season. Every farmer would have ten to fifteen burlap bags of newly shorn fleeces going to the Sheahey Yarn Mill at Phillips, and along would come the poor mailman in his buggy, his sleigh, or his Model T. "I'll have to come back," he'd call when he had so many bags tied on he couldn't sit down.

Things went fairly well, however, until the junk mail became a national evil. As a subscriber to a newspaper, I had my name sold to the mail-order industry and then things went to hell. My name is a property of great value. I get four identical catalogs in the same mail from Lillian Vernon, and three from L. L. Bean. The RFD carrier, now handling what is called a Highway Contract Route, tells me my newspaper went astray and is probably in Pemaquid, but he has seventeen catalogs, two batches of magazine sticker stamps, three checks for seven million dollars each, the usual questionaire from the Sierra Club, and two brochures from condominiums in Florida. It pleases me beyond belief that I pay twenty-nine cents to mail a letter, but all this stuff comes to me at "Bulk Rate Paid."

I recently received this letter:

Dear John,

What about junk mail?
Your suggestions might help.
Hastily,
Your only friend,
    (name withheld)

I shall not reveal the name of the penitentiary in Illinois from which this communication came. My answer follows:

Dear only friend,
On every hand I hear lamentation and vituperation about junk mail and how it has ruined things. But I do not complain—except that I am unhappy about being a "current resident," "postal patron," and "boxholder, local." Of course I am ripping mad at paying full prices when other people can reach me by "Pre-sorted" and pre-cancelled pittances. I dislike paying in full to take up the slack for a conglomerate that pays taxes in Nigeria but has postal privileges out of Evansville, Indiana. But I overlook all those things because of the envelopes.

Perhaps you didn't notice that. The envelopes? Every catalog and circular has a return envelope to make it easy for me to respond. If I need something from Drake's in Colorado, I just put my check in the "business reply" envelope—No Postage Required If Mailed in the USA. Now and then I mail one of these envelopes, but I don't put anything in it. The company has to pay, and it serves 'em right! Otherwise, I keep the envelopes and use them myself for personal purposes. I haven't bought an envelope since junk mail escalated.

I cross out whatever printing is on the envelopes with a felt pen, and then I use the Magazine Market Place or the Publishers Clearing House stamps to cover things like "Be Sure to Sign Your Check!" Have you priced a hundred No. 6 envelopes lately? Be glad for junk mail.

The catalogs don't burn readily, but if stood on edge rather than laid flat in the stove they will catch fire if stirred now and then with the poker. I save a lot on firewood in my little shop stove. If the weather is mild, I don't use any wood at all.

When do you get out?

Yours, etc.

I've found only one trouble with my recycled envelopes. I wrote to Joe Novick, asking him to make a date for our annual trout chowder, and I didn't hear from him. Joe got the letter, all right, but thought it was another offer from J. C. Penney and he tossed it in the trash. So I wrote again after a couple of weeks, and this time I recycled an envelope from L'Eggs Brand, Inc. This piqued Joe's curiosity, and he wrote me at once. And he also began recycling envelopes.

21 Camping Paper-Mill-Felt-Wise

Just as winter was gaining on us and I was hoping for a sedentary season with cribbage by the fire, some scoutmaster came on the radio with a stirring appeal for recruits, and said the program would include camping out "winterwise." Wisdom dictates otherwise, I say, and I assure one and all camping out winterwise is to be avoided if possible. In my stupid youth I used to do it, and stupidity can counteract many a discomfort. I found winter camping fully as invigorating as freezing to death, and a sport that can reasonably be compared to the hilarity of the Spanish Inquisition. But I—we—did not employ the word "winterwise." Did this scoutmaster mean camping out in the winter? Then why didn't he say so? Where do we get all these words like winterwise?

When you are introduced to a charming young lady and you have expressed joy at making her acquaintance, she may say, graciously and grammatically, "Likewise, I'm sure!" The adverbial suffix derives from *ways*, and comes up honorably in edgewise, lengthwise, endwise, sidewise, otherwise, likewise, and a few others that have been cheated out of all dignity by plethora of gobbledegook that gives us winterwise and syntax sins of that ilk. The banker offers advice securitywise. The baker says we should eat his bread healthwise. The town manager says things are tight taxwise, and futurewise we should expect increases. The schoolteachers, who should know better, complain salarywise. And when my neighbor Jim asked the handyman if he would begin picking up his trash every week, the handyman said he thought he could work Jim in all right Mondaywise.

Any scoutmaster who advocates winter camping should be returned to the asylum for rest and study, and further coaching in grammar if he needs it. Youthwise, I collected enough winter camping experience so now in later life I break out in goosebumps when an August heat wave drops into the low 90s. I shiver so dishes rattle in the cupboard. I was never a Boy Scout because at that time the movement had not reached my rustic retreat. But we boys did by instinct everything the Boy Scouts do for building character. I went winter camping because I knew no better, and we boys thought it was fun. If any prospective Boy Scout wishes to enroll because of winter camping, send him to me.

My favorite place was about a mile from the house and I would go there snowshoewise and pull my grub and gear tobogganwise. I did not take a shovel, because snow can be shoveled by a snowshoe. Before I set up my tent, I would build a fire. This was to thaw the tent so I could set it up. Sometimes I would cut two logs with my ax and lay them so I could tie my tent lines to them, but sometimes I would pound twenty-penny spikes into the frozen ground and use them for stakes. It took about the same time to drive the spikes as it did to cut two trees. After I got my tent up I would use a snowshoe to shovel snow against the canvas walls, all around except the front flap. Snowwise, this gives dandy insulation. By this time my fire would have the food thawed, and I could begin making supper. I always pushed four sticks into the snow and laid my toboggan across for a table. This was so I could dine sumptuously in great comfort.

Contrarywise to my spoofing, camping out in winter can be great fun if not pursued too assiduously. The fire and tent can be disposed so heat will radiate inside, and with snow insulation things stay reasonably warm and can, indeed, get stuffy. I never shook and shivered for more than a half hour when, drowsy, I crawled into my blanket. And, winterwise or summerwise, there's no need to have poor food off an outdoor fire. I got so I could pick up a bowl of delicious hot soup with my mittens on. So I suppose we boys who tented out in the good old winters could have passed any scouting merit badge test, even to roasting a rooster, if we'd known about such things.

And we did get along without any of the new-day privileges found, say, in the L. L. Bean catalog. Bedwise, for one thing, we had no interlined thermoproof sleeping bags, but had to make do with a thing called a "paper-mill felt." These could be had from paper mills, and were the cut-up sections of the great "webs" on a paper machine—the place where the paper starts in liquid form. After so many million miles of paper, the texture of the felt loses its nap and the whole thing must be replaced. The used felt, however, made dandy camp blankets, and the custom was to cut—tear, actually—it into squares, and every chopper in a Maine lumber camp had one. I was lucky along the line somewhere to become proprietor of a paper-mill felt about twelve feet square, and I could bed down in any snowbank and sleep comfywise. But before I got my felt the thing had been stained in the paper mill by a dye or an acid, so my blanket had a great splotch in the mid-portion that suggested I had wet my bed. When I draped my blanket over a tree limb to air or dry, the splotch could be seen for miles and I did get questioned about it. But that was my blanket and everybody knew it. In the dark, all blankets are the same color, and my biggest worry was about getting out of that blanket into the frigid Maine winter to replenish my fire. There was always one overpowering delight about winter camping. Morning came and I could go home. Earlywise.

22 Why Does Albert Have My Hat?

There came in the mail lately a request that I join sentient and righteous people in a Great Crusade to get English established as the official language of the United States of America. I was asked for a donation, too. Just about that time I was watching that television show, "Wheel of Fortune," and the puzzle was a phrase. Everybody guessed letters until somebody guessed the answer. When this "phrase," which paid off several thousand dollars, was shown on the screen, it turned out to be, "A man is known by the company he keeps." Yes, I think it would be a dandy idea if some language or another were established as official in the United States of America; and that folks be required to learn it and use it. Maybe a country is known by what it speaks. A man is known by the company he keeps!

Aristophanes quoted that; with credit to Euripedes, and Euripedes' dates were circa 485 to 406 B.C. Both those gentlemen, I betcha, could diagram sentences. Has anybody 'ceptin' me noticed the progressive erosion of the English language in the words of those who use it? The schoolmarm I had so long ago who led us budding grammarians along the pathway of erudition had a curious way of blowing on the end of her piece of chalk when she did anything at the blackboard. Her blackboard was black; now we have green blackboards! She'd pick up the piece of chalk, look at it to see if 'twere suitable for present purposes, and then point the business end of it at her mouth and puff. Pooph! To dust it off. At the beginning of the term, when we first saw her do this, we thought it an odd thing to do, but after a few days we caught on and whenever one of us was sent to the board we'd puff on the chalk the way she did. This mocking would set the class to giggling and tempered the boredom of scholarship.

If Mrs. Pratt noticed that we did this, she didn't let on and we had a roomful of chalk blowers. And, so many years later, I have a chalkboard in my workshop and every time I set down something to remind me I catch myself blowing on the chalk. I am thus reminded pleasantly of a gracious lady to whom I owe a great deal. As Mrs. Pratt encouraged us in the discovery of syntax, the early examples were simple: ALBERT HAS MY HAT. Albert is a proper noun and the subject of the sentence. Hat is the object. My is a possessive pronoun, and "my hat" becomes a predicate phrase. As easy as that, and the intricacies of sentence structure were inculcated. Puff by puff, Mrs. Pratt blew away a lot of chalk dust, and we youngsters found that dusting the chalk eases the tedium of culture. And as we went along the sentences got longer and trickier until one day, to show us we didn't know everything yet, Mrs. Pratt blew on her chalk and put up a sentence that ran the length of the blackboard twice and halfway again. We could see there is a difference between a word and a phrase, a phrase and a sentence. Mrs. Pratt's exemplary sentence was translated from somebody named Titus Livy, an author she said was extremely careful with his syntax, and she didn't expect us to diagram it. It was just something for us to think about. I copied the sentence and that night at home I tried to diagram it. The sentence was:

On the sixth day following the kalends Marcus Septus caused his standards to be displayed on the captured ramparts and sent his speediest messengers to the City, bringing news of his victory and his assurance that the menace of the Mendicanian pirates was ended, and upon the arrival of the messengers the citizens were stirred to public displays of gratitude and the Senate decreed a triumph for the day when Septus and his victorious legions should return.

You can see why that "phrase" on "Wheel of Fortune" made me think of Mrs. Pratt. I wished I might snap my fingers and set her on that show as a contestant, ready to blow on her chalk and tell the stupid producers that "A man is known by the company he keeps" is not a phrase.

So there may be a case for establishing English as our official national language—but who's going to teach it? Not long ago a man asked me how he should go about planning to build a house. I told him to buy a woodlot twenty-five years ago. Another day a woman asked me what her child should study in school so he'd grow up to be a writer. I told her to teach him to read Homer in the original Greek. The man and the woman both disregarded my excellent advice.

Then there was a schoolmarm, loaded with Educational qualifications, who said she didn't teach how to diagram a sentence as the children were supposed to have that before they came to her grade—"If they get it at all," she said.

Lumber is not cheap today, and cutting your own trees would make a house that much more attainable. If a child knows the *Iliad* and *Odyssey*, by that time he'll have a noggin so full of useful things he can write in his sleep. Bill Nye, considered so comical, outlined a course of study for the first School of Journalism. The classes went on and on for ninety-seven years, covering everything from the Law and papering a room to making a good adhesive paste that wouldn't sour in hot weather. The bloom of youth was tarnished by that time, but the student was ready— and he not only could read and write English, but could spell it.

Little boys and girls, if English is to be our national language, should go and find a teacher who blows on her chalk. That might be one way to tell a phrase from the back side of Elmer Keith's barn.

23 A Deadbeat in California

Fifty years or so ago Clevie Bickford had a contract to plow snow in four of five contiguous towns, and there came a whopper that his equipment couldn't handle. Clevie waded through the snow to the railroad station and got the morning train to Boston. Clevie was hardly dressed for the big city. He was wearing heavy woolen pants tucked into Maine lumberman's larrigans, with a heavy red-and-black checked mackinaw, and on his head the Scotch cap with the ear-floppers tied up—ready to be let down if needed. And, he hadn't shaved in days. He looked like the very thing he was—a down-Mainer.

In the display room out on Commonwealth Avenue the salesman showed him an Oshkosh with hydraulic lift for the blades, four speeds, and a heated cab. "The best we've got." Clevie asked if he could get it on the evening freight for Maine. And Clevie said, "How much?" The salesman, looking again at Clevie's rough attire, swallowed to gain time, and said, "Er, ah—have you spoken to our Mr. Smith?"

Clevie said he hadn't; why should he? Well, Mr. Smith was the credit manager. Clevie said, "What's-a-matter, ain't money no good in Boston?"

Clevie hauled out his wallet, counted out the $27,000, and returned to Maine. The Oshkosh arrived on the 8:30 A.M. freight, and by sundown every road was open.

I think back on Clevie and his financial situation every so often now that the Mr. Smiths of our great nation have got us all on credit cards. Well, I was cleaning up the workbench in my shop and found a check made out to my order for $1,000, at which I kicked up my heels and shouted goody-goody so the cat came out from under the shop stove and climbed the broom handle onto the bandsaw.

This is not my cat. I don't have a cat. I don't know whose cat this is. It has one blue eye and one green eye and a yank in the tail that suggests it failed, at least once, to pass before the door shut. I am not adicted to cats, being leery from memories of one that hated me long ago. That one was a she, and she'd lurk in wait behind the grain chest and attack me when I went for grain for bossy. She'd charge with a snarl and climb my overalls, wreaking havoc on the way, and I always had a quick thought that the Comanches had struck again. I never did get used to her. I tried to be kind, but she remained aloof. I was irked at her unrelenting hostility, and also by her agility at getting out of the way when I swung a pail at her. We just didn't have rapport. I moped about this and some folks thought I had a secret disturbance. Down the road the neighbors would hear this cat snarl and strike at me, and they'd say, "Oh, oh—there she goes again!"

So that cat tainted my life as regards cats, and in my old age I am happy to remain catless. Some nine miles from me, and across the river, lives a lovely lady who admires cats and I permit her to exude surrogate affection in my stead. She loves cats enough for everybody and wrote a book about cats. Cautiously, however, I take no public stand if asked about cats. People such as this lady who do love cats always love them very much, so I don't want a reputation for a disingratiating attitude. That I let this two-eyed cat use my shop tells a good deal about me.

She came in one day just two jumps ahead of Rudy Barter's hound, who had just chased her down from North Edgecomb. She loped into the shop and treed on my ten-foot stepladder. Rudy's dog is named Chum, so I said, "Chum, you old fool—get outa here and go home!" Then the cat came down and went under the stove, and she has lived under my stove ever since.

And I was some surprised that this cat took an interest when I found the check for $1,000 under the mess on my bench. I didn't suppose money meant anything to a cat.

This check didn't interest me quite that much. Well, I used to have a charge card for Amoco gasoline. I had cards for Gulf, Texaco, Mobil, and Exxon, too, but I never used the Amoco. We didn't have an Amoco pump around here, or at least I didn't know of one. I didn't play favorites—if I went that way I bought Gulf, and if I went the other I bought Exxon, and if there'd been an Amoco station I'd have bought Amoco. Somebody must have noticed that my Amoco card languished in innocuous desuetude, because I got this splendid communication from Associates National Bank of Pleasanton, California, which said it was replacing my inactive Amoco credit card with a genuine MasterCard—now I not only could buy Amoco gasoline with it, but I could also buy anything else everywhere in the world at five million places of business. They told me they had favored me by extending my credit line to $2,500, and enclosed I would find a check made out to me for $1,000 which I could apply to my heart's desire.

It just goes to show you what clean living will do.

This did seem to solve all my problems except where to find an Amoco station, but I was moody and brooded for a few days to think that after a successful career in my beloved Pine Tree State, owning some bank shares and a little real estate, I was pegged in California as a deadbeat after $2,500. I believe this disturbed the cat, too. All at once she realized that this prosperity was merely a come-on, and she had foolishly attached herself to a nobody. If I should cash this check, she realized, the $1,000 would go on my MasterCard and I would make easy monthly payments with 18 percent you-know-what. And now, having found this check amongst the stuff bound for our sanitary landfill, I looked again and found it was void after thirty days—that is, since last September. So much for Amoco.

But things like that in our new era of instant credit do make me think of Clevie Bickford, who always paid cash and took 2 percent. He died well-to-do, and lived the same way. But I did tack my check to the shop wall, to give my visiting cat a sense of security.

24 Here's My Two Cents' Worth

B eing of sound mind, I can recall when speaking up was known as "putting in your two cents' worth," and that's what it cost to mail a letter. That included delivery, too. When postage was hiked to twenty-nine cents, I put in my two cents' worth and implored the postal service to revert to old-time policy and introduce economy measures. Otherwise, postage will keep climbing until the national debt looks reasonable. But nobody listened to me, as usual, and propaganda has already commenced for the next increase.

My father was a railway postal clerk for forty-two years, riding back and forth from Bangor to Boston, so during my growing up I was well aware of the constant desire to "put the postal service on a sound basis." Dad would expound on all the things that might be done, and we'd sit at the dinner table listening to his remarks. He used to tell us how every department in the United States Government lived off the postal service. Everybody, then, got free seeds from his congressman, the seeds being provided by the Department of Agriculture. Congress would appropriate funds to pay the postage. The United States Customs House in Boston, he said, provided office space to just about every government department—immigration, forestry, banking, flood control, army recruiting, you name it. But because there was a sub-postal-station on the tenth floor the entire upkeep of the building was charged off to the postal service. Then Congress made up the deficits. The ways the postal service got milked were many and devious. Dad liked to tell about the merchant marine subsidy.

The United States never subsidized its merchant marine, although every other country in the world did. We got around this by mail contracts. Anything that floated and would sport Old Glory on the taffrail could get a mail contract. Mail was transported at sea by the mile, not by the ton. If a skipper was leaving New Orleans for Boston with baled cotton, he would go to the New Orleans post office and mail himself a picture postcard to general delivery, Boston. Then he would go back to his vessel and wait for a truck to bring him a pouch of mail that contained only his own postcard to himself. The postal service paid him, or his owners, just as much per mile for that one postcard as he'd get if he'd had his hold full of mail. But, you see, the United States never subsidized its merchant marine. On the other hand, the postal service did some curious bookkeeping. The same thing happened with the railroads, and the airlines. All the years my father worked the railway mail, he was cramped into a thirty-foot car—the other half of the sixty-foot car was carrying baggage for the railroad. And, all those years, the postal service paid for a sixty-foot car. And Congress picked up the tabs so postage stayed at two cents.

Those were the good old days.

The truth, carefully concealed, was that the postal service never had a deficit. It had parasites. To divert attention, every so often there would be an economy move, meant to put things in order so the price of stamps wouldn't go up. One such, in my time, had to do with cotton string. For long years a package of letters—a "packet"—was tied in transit by a cheap jute twine that was used once and disposed of. Every sorting clerk had a special knife for cutting this twine off a package when he came to handle it, and the severed twine was allowed to fall on the floor. Swept up, it was burned. This was the cheapest way to bundle letters, but congressmen from the southern states came up with a better idea. They wangled things until the postal service changed to cotton string. The pitch was that this would help the poor southern cotton farmers, and in the long run would save the taxpayers millions. It would also hold postage at two cents.

Postal clerks had a way of tying off a package of letters with one hand. Hold the letters, as picked from a pigeonhole in the sorting case, in the left hand, wind the string with the right and tie the knot with two fingers. Every clerk learned to do this on his first day, and it became automatic—a clerk could do it in his sleep. Then, making a loop around his right forefinger, the clerk would jerk the tied-up packet of letters in such a way that it severed the string from the ball. The jute twine was no stronger than that.

So now, to keep expenses down, cotton twine appeared and there was no more jute. The day cotton twine appeared, the postal service got 78,000 applications for temporary disability. Every clerk had tied off his first packet and tried to break the string over his finger. The cotton string didn't break worth a hoot. And you can't sort letters with your forefinger in a sling. So jute string came back and the southern cotton farmers went on relief. And postage went up to three cents.

A truly great effort to cut down postal expenses was made during the administration of President William Howard Taft. President Taft appointed Frank H. Hitchcock of Massachusetts the postmaster general and told him (the usual instructions) to put the postal service on a paying basis. Postmaster General Hitchcock went right to work. It had long been customary for postal clerks to keep their records in "indelible" pencil. The ballpoint pen was far up ahead, and at that time the fountain pen was unreliable. An indelible pencil made a mark that could not be erased, if a clerk was minded to make some changes. So Postmaster General Hitchcock observed that a clerk would use an indelible pencil until it got shorter and shorter, and then he would throw away the stub and get a new pencil. Aha! Every clerk was given a little tin ferrule that would fit over a short pencil and extend it for further use. Now pencils were used right down to the veriest stub and countless thousands of dollars were saved. There seems to be no public record of what the ferrules cost. Postage went up again. But in the mail service, a pencil came to be called a hitchcock, and there came a day when none of the postal clerks could remember why. Frank Hitchcock was long forgotten, even though he lent his name to postal economy. My mother, who greatly outlived my father, celebrated her hundredth birthday—possibly the last living person to remember either Hitchcock or two-cent letters.

There's no need to leave such valiant efforts at postal solvency in the forgotten past. The postal people should think up things all over again. They probably will never get us back to a three-cent letter, but we deserve to be amused.

25 The Policeman's Lot— Not Happy

An appealing letter came not long ago to my appealing wife, asking her to donate liberally to a fund that will erect a memorial in the District of Columbia to law enforcement officers. This is probably all right, but the appeal says it has the support of our Friendship Police Department, and Friendship doesn't have any police department. We should be ashamed of ourselves, but that's the way things stand. We should do better than that in this dreary age when crime is running away with itself and the constabulary is undermanned, underpaid, and underesteemed.

This appeal came from United States Senator Al D'Amato, who says he is honorary chairman of the fund raising committee. He urges my wife to contribute while there is yet time. He says he has worked hard in the Senate to make sure criminals get caught and punished. My wife, who has not yet mailed a check, says she is all for that and she hopes he catches every criminal in the Senate and they all get punished. She asked me if I thought she should write a letter to Senator D'Amato and tell him of the great sadness that befell our clam warden in the prosecution of his sworn duty.

It is true that our coastal town of Friendship, a fishing harbor midway of the Maine tide, has no police department. We do have a harbor master who amounts to a policeman for the waterfront, but some days he has nothing to do and plays cribbage with the Maytag repairman. Our harbor master gets paid five hundred dollars a year whether he does anything or not, and the comfort of knowing he's on duty is worth every penny. He is not really an expense on the taxpayer, as his stipend comes from the excise tax on boats. So the fishermen who use the harbor pay for their own policing and everybody seems happy with this arrangement. If you ever come into our snug little Friendship harbor with your beautiful summer mahogany, you'll do well to hunt up Blake Wotton first thing. He's our harbor master. He'll show you where to drop your killick and might even find you a mooring. He can show you where the town landings are, so you can tie up and come ashore. But we don't think of Blake as being a police officer. Fact is, Friendship doesn't even have a constable.

Most towns that don't have policemen have a constable. He's the basic enforcement officer of the Maine system, low man down the line. He can make arrests if he wants to, but usually doesn't, and he can serve papers. If he does serve papers, the most important one is the annual call for town meeting. The selectmen prepare the agenda and then give the "warrant" to a constable. The constable "notifies and warns" the inhabitants that town meeting is coming up by posting the warrant in "public and conspicuous" places. Then he makes a "return" to the town clerk, saying he has posted the warrant, and we're in business.

Our Maine courts have ruled that this "posting" by the constable is the big thing in our system of local government, so the constable does have his importance. But Friendship doesn't have one; our warrant is posted by "a citizen." In late years, in Friendship, this citizen has been Roger Bramhall, who is just as good as any constable and, probably, better.

You musn't get the idea Friendship is without crime. We've had rascals. One time years ago a lawyer said that Hunky Todd was a "felon," and Tiddle Coombs, who was a witness in the trial, said that wasn't so. He said Hunky may have robbed the bank all right, ". . . but he ain't no felon!" But we do have a high percentage of upright, pious, and respectable people (we have only eight hundred people of all persuasions) and lawlessness is low. Once in a while somebody may keep a short lobster, and once we had a juvenile who swiped a hub cap. But honest felons are rare. If, once in a blue moon, we need a peace officer, we are not bereft. Within call and handy are game and forest wardens, the county sheriff and his deputies, marine wardens, and the somewhat elusive state police. The forest warden, or ranger, looks for woods fires and gives advice about logging off lumber. The game warden looks for poachers, and three years ago found one. Woodrow Blackington had poached a moose in August and didn't realize the beast had been fitted with a telltale radio transmitter on a collar around the neck. Woodrow was just starting to skin the moose when the warden arrived. The marine warden looks for short lobsters, inspects sardines, and goes down twice a day to call in the tide. Also clam wardens, who are named by the town instead of the state. And then the state police—but I don't know much about them. One evening my wife and I were sent off the road into the ditch by a reckless driver, and I telephoned to the state police barracks in some perturbation. A lady answered and said she was just going off duty and I should call in the morning. She suggested it would be well if I made an appointment. She said she was sorry. I suppose if I really needed a peace officer in any kind of a dire emergency, I would call the High Sheriff. He holds an elective office, and needs my vote.

So we manage, and now Senator D'Amato will want to hear about the great sadness that befell our clam warden. Clam diggers need a town license and must never dig in "closed" flats. Now and then a section of the shore will be off-limits for conservation reasons—let the little clams grow up. It goes pretty hard on a digger caught on closed flats. So Friendship named a new clam warden who was all eager and keen-eyed. The morning he was sworn in, new on the job, he went on a prowl and almost immediately encountered a clam digger who was breaking the law. It broke his heart, but he was obliged to arrest his own brother. Such honest prosecution deserves attention and support, and if Senator D'Amato will include our clam warden in his Washington memorial, I'll send him ten dollars. Or, let my wife do it.

26 Everybody Have More Children!

There is little hilarity in the great changes in Maine real estate. Not even in the 1990 census form, which came in the morning mail and got sent back that afternoon. We are just two, and we have no aggravated problems. I filled the form out and had done with it. Not a laugh. Then in a week or so my cheerful co-owner answered the telephone to be told that I hadn't answered all the questions. My co-owner handles such things astutely, so she said, "Oh?"

"Yes," the lady-person voice said, "you didn't put down the value of your property if offered for sale." So if you ask what's happened to things around here, that's one answer. My wife said, "That's right!"

It's a great pity to have this absurdity given dignity by official Washington, D.C. The question deserves hilarity, but nobody is inclined to smile. Do other states have this complaint? I didn't answer that question on the census form because there isn't any answer, and if I should feign one it's no business of the boys in D.C. Here in Maine since 1820 real estate taxes have been collected by the town on the basis of values locally assessed, and each year the figures are printed in our town reports. Anybody can look at our town reports, including the secretary of commerce in Washington, who takes the census.

In recent years, the basic Maine consideration that land was to be lived on and homes were to be lived in has eroded into this preposterous fantasy that everything is for sale. Frantic desires by well-heeled out-of-staters to get away from hectic city life and achieve serenity amidst scenery have had their effect. Some clown with more money than brains comes along and pays $200,000 for a half-acre of seaside ledge, and then spends as much again to put up a cottage. This has become the new-day gauge of values, and henceforth every ledge within ten miles is appraised, and assessed, at $400,000 an acre. The landed gentry of the vicinity, ordinary Maine folks who farm and fish, and cut pulpwood, or write pleasantly for the journals, didn't realize they were so flushed with wealth. They have suddenly become the richest bankrupts in America. They, like me, just wanted to live the way they were, and as their forebears were.

I haven't the slightest notion of selling my property. By any honest appraisal, mine is not an expensive place to own. I have little tied up in it. I did most of the carpentry. I am not on the waterfront. I have no special view. I am not on a public way. I plow my own snow and I am not on a public sewer. Our children are long out of school. I have just about an acre of land. I am not "commercial." I pump my own water. The purpose of our real estate is simple—my wife and I hope to abide pleasantly and listen to our arteries harden along with the best that's yet to be. But the imaginary "value" of our little place jumps like a skyrocket every time some nut from Massachusetts pays $75,000 for some shore swamp in the vicinity.

The accredited economist who eventually gets a big government grant to study this transition and evaluate its effects will want to look closely at our School Administrative Districts—properly abbreviated to "SAD." They have much to do with this "selling price" addiction. In the beginning Maine schools were strictly a home-town affair—each town handled its own education and schools "kept" in local school districts. The district schoolhouse was more than an institution of learning. Parents used it for social occasions, and parents went to regular meetings when their children "recited." School and home were close. People took "education" seriously. Remember what the father did when his boy came home from school and said the teacher spanked him? The old man was furious. He hitched the horse to the buggy and rode pell-mell to the schoolhouse, catching the teacher just before she stepped out and locked the door for the day.

"My Jimmie says you spanked him!"

"Yes, I did," the teacher admitted. "He was inattentive and unruly, and he sassed me."

"Well, by God, Ma'am—don't you never do such a thing again! You tell me, and I'll whup him. I'm stronger than you be!"

One by one the little rural schools closed, and the bus was invented. Education took on a capital E—Education. With each change the home became farther away, until today a parent who tries to "take an interest in the schools" might as well whistle into the wind. And then the professional educators thought up the "consolidated" high school, and here we are today.

Local taxpayers no longer vote in town meeting on their school funds. They get no explanations—at least any they can understand and relate to. The state, distant and money-seeking, has developed a "formula" for school funds. Our little town of

Friendship, sucked into a School Administrative District back in the days when some people supposed they were good, pays every year to put thirty children through high school (located in another town!) and sends only six. It is absolutely true that when questioned about this, an "expert" sent around by the state house said our solution was to breed more children, until by numbers we got what we were paying for. Person, time, and place are on · record. And, it isn't funny.

In times gone by, town assessors were kind to older folks living on family places. Assessors knew it was cheaper for a town to make concessions than it would be to support the old couple in a "home." So assessments were gentle until the old folks "got through." Today, the Old Higgins Place, where Jim and Beulah Higgins live, is no longer considered as a family home, where a pleasant old couple can spend their last comfortable days, but is appraised at eighty house lots, an acre apiece, at $85,000 an acre, and even more for a shopping mall. Don't laugh; Maine has a lot of Higginses.

So I didn't fill in that blank. We're not selling.

27 We Could Do Much Worse

Somewhere, lately, I ran across a reference to Gypsies, and it was uncomplimentary. Gypsies used to come to Maine and I inherited an admiration for them from my grandfather. The only time I, myself, had dealings with Gypsies they were decent people, and I waved at them, and they at me, as they disappeared in caravan up the road. I haven't seen a Gypsy in Maine since.

Grandfather's liking for Gypsies stemmed from trading horses. Back in the days just after the Civil War, the roving Gypsies depended on horse trading instead of their stereotyped fortune telling and trickery. When people tell about stealing and cheating, they are talking about later times; Grandfather said they were scrupulously honest and could be trusted. When my grandfather received his soldier's bonus from the state, he pondered what to do with this windfall. And he asked the next band of roving Gypsies what it might do for him in the way of a Morgan filly.

Without the slightest question, my grandfather was the most proficient horse trader in Maine. With him, as with all accomplished horse traders, dishonesty was recognized along with other moral philosophies, a laudable virtue when two farmers stood face to face in a hoss swap. An element of sharpie sportsmanship mitigated the prevaricating; expected. Falsehood was window-dressing, an inverted kind of truth. My grandfather was best known about the countryside for the truthful way he beguiled Sime Coombs about Garabaldi. Garabaldi was a "green" white stallion Grandfather had acquired when he needed a new horse for haying and had no time to be choosy. He was stuck with Garabaldi and Sime Coombs offered a good chance to work him off. He told Sime, "Now, Sime, I don't want to put nawthin' over on you about this fine hoss, so I'm going to admit to you fair and square that he's got two faults. I'll tell you out of hand what his first fault is, and if we trade I'll tell you the other."

Sime said, "What's his first fault?"

Gramp said, "Well, he's awful hard to catch."

That's no great fault. If a horse is hard to catch you just don't turn him loose. So Sime decided to take Garabaldi and he said, "What's his other fault?"

As Gramp tucked the money in his wallet and put the wallet in his pocket he said, "He ain't no good once you catch him."

But, Grandfather told me, that kind of hoss-tradin' equivocation was taboo when the Gypsies came. The next spring after he'd spoken to the Gypsies about a Morgan filly, King Harry of the Gypsies swirled his caravan and his remuda into our dooryard and singled out a beautiful Morgan filly. Gramp fell in love. Morgans were not that common in Maine then, and Gramp felt a brood mare was a good way to invest his bonus. King Harry said the filly was sound and clever, and stated the price. If King Harry said so, that was all right with Gramp. They didn't haggle.

That Morgan dropped a foal regularly for almost thirty years. She was one of my grandfather's wisest investments. The colts he offered for sale were but half Morgan, but they all sold quickly and fetched their price. Now and then the Gypsies would buy one, and they always paid Gramp's price and took his word. Nobody else would. "Gypsies are honest traders," he told me once. "They make good friends." He never said as much about Horace Jordan, Sylvanus Malm, Jedeniah Bickford, or anybody else that lived along our road.

By my time, the last foal that Morgan mare had produced was coming up to twenty-five years or so. I hated the thing and she hated all humanity save Gramp. She was mean and nasty and could spit like a camel. She was absolutely worthless and a menace about the place. She was a crowder, and bit and kicked, and only Gramp could lay a hand on her. She was his pet, the last colt of the beautiful Morgan mare he'd bought with his war money. She was a reminder of the days that were. From the day she was born he called her Colty.

He knew from that day that he would never part with her. She lived to be thirty and never knew a bridle or halter. He'd step from the house of a summer morning and call, "Colty— here Colty!" and from wherever she was on the farm she'd come lacing to his side to get her ears rubbed and her cube of sugar. Except to amuse Grandfather, she served no purpose. She lived in idle luxury. She loved only the Old Soldier.

By the time Colty was well along, Gypsies ceased to trade in horses and stopped coming. When they did come, they had automobiles and bad reputations. They cheated and stole, so it was said, and were not welcome. It got so, along in the 1920s, that bands of Gypsies would be met at a town line and escorted on through to the next town. King Harry, legendary for a generation, was long gone, but he must have passed along some Gypsy lore to his descendants. One summer a Gypsy caravan came to our town and the chief of police started to escort it through. But it turned off at our driveway, and before the police chief missed it the whole caravan was set up in the field behind our barn. The Gypsies all waved as they passed me in the dooryard. They stayed in our field for three days. The chief of police told me I was foolish, that they'd rob me blind, and I should let him move them along. I thought of Grandfather and the Morgan filly—and foolish Colty—and I said I'd take my chances.

After three nights the caravan moved on just after sunrise. I was coming out of the house and I waved back at them. I haven't seen any Gypsies in Maine since—but sometimes I think we could do worse than cultivate Gypsies.

28 An Unconstitutional Summer?

To arms ye gentlemen! It is February as I meditate, and February in Maine is ideal for meditation. And this time, we can meditate about Indian Summer, which is wonderful for February meditations. You must realize the emergency—we have been enjoying Indian Summer for all these many beautiful times, year after joyous year, and we may never enjoy it again! For the moment, the Feminists have lost the battle and we simple men-folks who like our Indian Summers can take heart. But the war goes on! To arms!

It was in my favorite outlander newspaper, the Esslinger *Zeit-ung*, and it said a big lawsuit is rampaging in the German courts demanding the abolition of Indian Summer. I'll try to explain it, so listen carefully:

As we decent Mainers well know, Indian Summer is at best a nebulous, tenuous, illusive, and even whimsical interlude which may or may not appear on schedule. If we have Indian Summer, unseasonably warm air, usually dry, visits our part of the United States and Canada. True Indian Summer has a soft haze that mellows the scenery. It is a delicious dividend, easing off the severity of our vicious northeast line storm to make way for the rigors of the first blizzard of winter. Indian Summer is a lot like the hyphen in ROWDY-DOW! The next thing will be Christmas. But Indian Summer is special because it belongs to us—that is, the tourists are gone. Indian Summer is too good for them. So we can sit comfy by the fire in February and consider Indian Summer. Indian Summer is like velvet to burlap. A caress to a slap. It fleets and is gone. And now the Women's Lib has struck again, and as the winter wind whistles "Yankee Doodle" through the keyhole a German newspaper tells us Indian Summer is unsporting.

As I think back on the Indian Summers I have known, per-haps my happiest memory has to do with lining bees. Here in Maine, where anything we pay a legislator is altogether too much, the jokers made lining bees illegal some years ago. It is a high crime to line a bee in Maine. But I lined bees in Indian Summer as a boy, before anything much was illegal, and I'm glad. Some-body told me some summer resident caught somebody lining a bee on his precious property, and he didn't like being tres-passed against. Eager to please all summer residents, the legis-lature responded. No doubt in the good old days, before Summer People, an occasional wild tree full of comb honey would get chopped down by somebody lining bees, and this was naughty, but instead of making it unlawful to chop down a summercater's bee tree, the legislature wisely outlawed lining bees. The tail goes with the hide. The way I lined bees in Indian Summer, I never chopped a tree.

I'd make a little box with a glass cover, put in a dab of comb honey, and fare into the countryside looking for a comfortable glade in which to assume a recumbent posture. I would arrange myself to take complete advantage of Indian Summer. The golden rod is usually waning by Indian Summer, but the fall asters are rampant and because the year is running out the bees are working every aster blossom for what they can get. Accordingly, I select a comely bee and put him into my little box with the honey, and I close the glass cover so he can't fly away until I let him. Then I watch my bee through the glass. He takes a moment to look things over and decide on a course, and upon finding the honey he kicks up his little heels in joy and starts to feed. You'll notice I keep referring to my captive bee as "he." The feminists won't win this one! The worker bee is neuter; my "he" is an "it." So it kicks up its little heels. After it has filled its equipment with my honey, it is ready to fly to the hive and deposit it, and I can watch this through the glass. When I lift away the cover, off the bee goes in what is often called a bee line. He makes a circle or two, to get his bearings, and nature has fixed him so he—it—goes straight for home. All the while I am lolling back in the beauty of Indian Summer, glad for everything and mad at nobody.

I would gladly explain how I pick a red-hot honeybee off an aster blossom and put him into my little box, but since it is now a crime to line bees I shall not become accessory to a felony. But it can be done without any great threat to public safety. The length of time my bee takes to fly home, discharge his free honey, and return to the box for more will tell me about how far away his colony is. (I mean it; not he.) And when it returns, the bee will have some friends with it—other bees suspect it is on a gravy train and follow it. And in turn, other bees will follow each follower. In this way a line of bees in flight extends shortly from my little box to the hollow tree, or hive, and if I wanted to I could walk along looking up and follow the flight. But this was always indolent fun for me, and as we always kept bees anyway I had no need to hunt wild honey. Fact is that most of the bee lines I started went to one of my own colonies anyway. After I'd finished my sandwiches, and maybe had a nap in the warm Indian Summer sun, I'd rouse and go home—leaving my little box so the bees could clean up my honey. So here we are in February, and that's the way I was thinking.

Now, according to the Esslinger *Zeitung*, Indian Summer is not called Indian Summer in the German language. Germans seem to have a similar spell of weather, but they spell it *Altweibersommer*, which translates as Old Woman's Summer. And as the quest for female equality accrued, somebody with nothing better to do in February hired a lawyer and went to court to get the government weather bureau people to stop saying *Altweibersommer*. The word was insulting, the lawyer said, to a substantial part of the German population. It was derogatory and demeaning. The judge was told that every time the weather bureau said *"Altweibersommer"* all the elderly females in the *Bundesgebiet* had a rising gorge and felt just terrible. Unless the court gave relief, there was no telling what the old women of Germany might do. They (the *Altweibervolk*) must be freed of this stigma and discourtesy.

We can take heart that this first effort was repulsed. The judge denied a restraining order, and held that the word *Altweibersommer* was traditional and beyond recall. He said it never did carry any inappropriate meaning. Good for the judge, but these people who want to reform everything are persistent. Mark my words! They'll be back, and one day we'll see the Supreme Court siding with the Old Ladies, love 'em! The day will come when some Indian will jump up and tell us Indian Summer is unconstitutional.

29 It Isn't That Easy to Get

And here is this kind letter from Donald Mainwaring in another state who tells of his student days in Scotland when he hied the harried haggis o'er the Doon and watched auld Ben Lomond toss the caber across Loch Bagel. He says the finest-flavored potatoes ever to grace his gullet were grown in Ayrshire on seaweed fertilizer, and he wonders why we, up to our ears in Maine seaweed, don't use it on our potato farms. Aye, laddie.

A-weel, a-weel, Mon, the truth is that I want no better taties than the Green Mountains I grow in my backyard on barnyard encouragement, laced by a slap of 5-10-10. I refer Mr. Mainwaring to his library for another look at that wise short tale by Nathaniel MacHawthorne, "The Birthmark," which didacticates about perfecting perfection. As Bobbie Burns so well put it whilst plowing in Ayrshire, mickel a muckel mookles a wheedly tardle. Just take ain o' my lovelies, gie it an unco bake, add a daud o' butter, and then ask what the poor people in the Heelands are eating! Seaweed, indeed.

On the other hand, seaweed—rockweed in Maine—does have a salubrity when applied to sass, and we in Maine know that well. More than one Highlander, and Lawlander, too, came to Maine in the early days to cut the fish, and they felt at home immediately along our rugged coast with its background of hills. A good Maine granite ledge is as good as any peat-reeking croft in Glen Uig, and our early settlers found the quickest way to sprout a seed was to lay it on a rock and cover it with seaweed.

"Just like home!" said every Scot in Maine as he creeled his rock-weed along the shore. Potato cuttings laid along the ledge and bedded down with seaweed would sprout with vigorous intent. As mulch, rockweed held the rain, caught the sun, held down weeds, and as decomposition accrued it nourished the crop. No plowing, no harrowing, no cultivating, no hoeing, no weeding. A lad could lay down his garden, spend the summer handlining The Bank and come home to find his taties ready to dig. Except that they didn't get dug. Just pull away the seaweed, and there are the potatoes lined up on the ledge waiting to be gathered. All this is old stuff in Maine gardening.

Rockweed at sea gets churned about by the storms and by the tides, and broken off parts drift ashore. Every spring a high-water-mark windrow of rockweed lines the coast of Maine and of the offshore islands. With a pitchfork, a man can quickly gather enough for his kitchen garden. When added to the soil, rock-weed breaks down easily and makes excellent humus. But it would be for gardens nigh the tide. Aroostook County, which is Maine's potato empire, lies much too far inland to allow prac-tical use of seaweed. Which is probably good, because coastal flavors are not always relished by highlanders (or flatlanders) and a few hundred acres of biodegradable rockweed moist and active under an Aroostook sun would exert a bracing effluvium that would prove objectionable in Fort Fairfield. I guarantee it. Down at the shore a small potato patch, just for family use, will advertise its seaweed potency so crows will fly out around. By the shore, such olfactory exuberance is acceptable, and tourists call it ozone and consider it healthy and invigorating. Seaweed fertilizer is not used much in built-up places, and would make a home gardener unpopular.

And there's something else that needs consideration in this day and age. Much of the coast of Maine and a good part of the islands have passed into the possession of summercaters, and we natives have eased off on our traditional and residual cus-toms. There isn't a seasonal, nonresident taxpayer from Kittery Point to Quoddy Head who has the slightest use or need for rockweed, except maybe to cover an occasional clambake, but the appearance of somebody down on the beach raking rockweed would promote a howl beyond belief. Summercaters are possessive, even though ownership ceases at high-water mark, right where rockweed begins. Nobody owns the ocean. But let a gardener come to gather a wheelbarrow of rockweed, to which he is absolutely entitled even if he gardens ten miles inland, and he'll hear soon enough, "And just what do you think you're doing?" If an Aroostook potato farmer really wants to experiment with rockweed fertilizer, he'll do well to rent a barge and find an uninhabited island somewhere around 43-51-30; 68-53-30. That would make seaweed expensive, and we're right back where we started—barn manure and 5-10-10.

30 Black Cat—A Reformed Methodist

N ow take the coon cat—which people do. There was a time the Maine Coon Cat sat on back steps and carried on the traditions of Bast, minding his cat's business and giving all the dogs a hard time. Somewhere along the line he got stylish and became a prized and honored beast. All at once we had Maine Coon Cat Clubs and cat buffs all over the place, and life in Maine changed. People who used to put signs out by the road that offered free kittens found they could get paid for the things, and happy tourists took Maine Coon Cats back to coon-catless states believing they had something special. There's a lady over in the next town who has written a book about Maine cats. Good! But as an expert on cats from away back, I think Maine was better off when we just left the things on the doorsteps with the general agreement that cats should walk alone and all places were the same. Today, there's agitation to license cats, and keep them on leashes like a dog. Maybe they'll be belled!

The last cat I kept, which was long ago and I'm glad, was a reformed Methodist, which is a local joke. He was black, and we called him Black Cat. There's a place yonder that used to have a Methodist fervor, with a big white church to match, and where the two range roads crossed became known as Methodist Corner. Sundays, Methodists would come for miles by horse and buggy, and except for a steeple the horse sheds were bigger than the church. This persuasion in that locality dwindled in time, but the area continued to be Methodist Corner, and even today, so long after Black Cat, it still is. Our good friends, Alex and Joyce Hall, lived by that crossroads (in Maine that's a four-corners) and they kept a few cats in the original and respectable Maine style. Most of their cats were Coon Cats, except sometimes. The true Maine Coon Cat is supposedly descended from Persian varieties brought home aboard ship as mousers by old Maine blue-water sailors. No reason to doubt this. Cats, as promiscuity accrues, have a way of reproducing characteristics regardless of parentage. Every once in a while, the same old cat will show up again, regardless of planned parenthood. At the time now in focus, many years back, we were using the services of a reliable and adequate female Manx that caused no problems in the neighborhood and kept fairly Christian hours. Stubby was her name, for as a Manx she was stub-tailed. The Manx does make a useful cat once you get so you can stand a cat, but apart from that Stubby gave me the chance to use my old jest, namely, that we keep a stub-tailed cat because she takes less time to go through a door on a cold day. A long-tailed cat who likes to have the door held open for her while she takes her own good time to pass can be measured in BTU's, and should not be encouraged. Any cat with a long tail that tried to live with us learned to come in or go out with alacrity, and otherwise had a yank. Even Stubby knew that a dilly-dally was unwise. But one day Stubby wore out in her indefatigable attention to our necessities, and we needed a replacement. Joyce Hall told us we could have either one or two dozen—it was all the same to her—and promised to help us catch however many we decided upon.

But as Stubby had persuaded us in favor of stub-tailed cats we mentioned that desire, and Joyce said at the moment she was fresh out, but that if we would wait a time with patience . . . She said it wouldn't be too long and she would be in touch.

I do hope I have made the point that there are two ways to keep a cat. One is this new-day belief that a cat needs patent food, must be licensed and held on a string, must have a beddy-bye basket by the cozy fire, and is valuable property worth the vet's fee and public esteem. The old-fashioned way, which takes notice of the nature of cats and their intended functions, is the way cats would ask to be treated if they had the vote. It's the way cats lived back when they sat on back steps and people gave them away. The numerous cats of Joyce and Alex Hall could go nine miles in one direction and ten in another, and if one of them neglected to show up there was nobody to stand in the door and call kitty-kitty-kitty. This sort of disinterest makes a cat happy, and one aspect of cat happiness is emphasized by the appearance now and then of a lovely Maine Coon Cat with no tail. Such a Maine Coon Cat can easily be passed off as a Manx. Joyce reported to us that we might come any time and get our stub-tailed cat.

As she promised, Joyce helped me catch him. She poured some warm milk in a dishpan and set the pan on the shed steps. Instantly, there was a wild charge like a Wagnerian horse-trot and cats came from all directions. One of them was our handsome black gentleman with his abbreviated eschatology. Joyce grabbed him by the scruff of his neck while he did a pinwheel with his legs, and after he simmered down she thrust him into a grain bag. When I got him home he spoke to me with a broad range of contumely, and took up residence on the kitchen rocking chair that used to be mine before B.C. (Black Cat). Whenever Black Cat left the chair on his missionary work about the acreage, I could use it. If he came into the house and found me in his

IT IS NOT NOW

chair, he would make coarse and pointed remarks. I wish Black Cat might be around today to mount a podium and state his opinion of cats that wear collars and sleep on pillows in the front room.

One time we went away for a few days and arranged with a boy down the road to come up every morning and feed Black Cat. When we got home the boy told us he fed Black Cat regularly, but hadn't laid eyes on him. The food he put out was eaten, but he hadn't seen Black Cat. But Black Cat appeared as soon as we unlocked our door, and with him ten or fifteen cats, including two that belonged to the boy down the road. All were fat and happy. Now that Black Cat began eating in the house again, his friends went away. He would sit in my chair and purr.

That's the way it is with cats, and I don't believe it's going to change. They operate best in a wide and spacious environment, and the fact that they come without tails now and then is proof that cat lovers don't really know all that goes on. I admit I never truly cared much for Black Cat, but I did treat him as a cat. He deserved that.

31 The Night Reggie Bouchard Spoke

A friend invited me to attend a luncheon of his gentleman's club, which I did. There was a candidate running for something, and after we ate he got up and told us he stood for clean living, more rain for the farmers, and prosperity. That seems to be what a gentleman's club amounts to, today, and maybe I should tell what a gentleman's club was like before improvement set in. Things have changed. Take, for instance, the evening that Reggie Bouchard came to talk to our Lobster Club, No. 1. Reggie did publicity for the Maine Department of Sea & Shore Fisheries and we thought it might be exciting to have him speak about our favorite subject. The Lisbon Lobster Club, No. 1, was formed in 1911 for the sole purpose of exterminating the Maine Lobster gastronomically. The club has met on the first Friday of every month ever since, being accordingly older even than Rotary, and I have been an honorary member (attained only by age) for many years. Totally unready for our Lobster Club, Reggie enjoyed his lobster and then gazed in awe as the meeting opened.

Immediately after President Al Stowe called the meeting to order I made the customary motion that we do now adjourn. This motion was passed unanimously, and then we had the secretary's report of the previous meeting. Secretary Irving McIntosh, making this report, included this: "Upon motion of Bill Spear, the treasurer's report was accepted as read."

Usually, our secretary's report is accepted after no more than twenty or twenty-five minutes of debate, and any deviation from the meticulous is severely dealt with. Irving, accordingly, is always careful. Sometimes, just to be sure, the club will refer the report to a committee of the ten eldest members for study. On this occasion, after Secretary McIntosh had seated himself, Member Bill Spear addressed the president and said he had not been present at the previous meeting. In some pertubation Secretary McIntosh said, "Are you sure?"

At this, Treasurer Melbourne W. Smith stated that he had not given any report at the previous meeting.

President Stowe interjected that he found it hard to believe these worthy members, since he had just heard the facts affirmed in the secretary's report. Secretary McIntosh nodded.

(Mr. McIntosh was our town's postmaster, and that very day he was walking home for lunch when an automobile stopped at the curb and the driver leaned out to ask Postmaster McIntosh, "Pardon me, sir, but could you tell me where Postmaster McIntosh lives?" Postmaster McIntosh said, "Certainly—in the little house up ahead, just this side of the church." The motorist said thank-you and was waiting in the dooryard when Postmaster McIntosh got home.)

The function of the treasurer of the Lobster Club, No. 1, is to divide the cost of the evening's lobster by the number of members attending, and to collect the money and give it to the official chef. The by-laws are strict about this. When the annual appeal from the Red Cross comes in the mail, a motion is always made that it be marked paid and deposited in the archives. The Lobster Club, No. 1, has never trusted its treasurers. Mr. Smith, in particular, often refused to read a report on the grounds that nobody listened.

President Stowe called for a motion that would resolve this matter of accepting a report that wasn't given upon motion by a member who wasn't there. Amel Kisonak, Sergeant at Arms, obliged—making a motion that for parliamentary purposes only Bill Spear be called present at the previous meeting, by unanimous consent.

At this, Treasurer Smith called attention to the fact that if Bill Spear is voted as present, he will be obliged to pay the supper assessment of $2.55.

Bill Spear then offered an amendment that the word "not" be inserted in the motion. President Stowe rejected the amendment on the grounds it changed the wording without changing the import and had a nugatory effect. Secretary McIntosh asked how to spell nugatory. In the end, the members voted that Smith did give a report, Spear moved to accept it, and Spear's assessment should be paid out of the contingent fund. Secretary McIntosh stated that he thought this was a good way to do things. The vote was two hundred in favor and three opposed. (Membership in Lobster Club, No. 1, is limited to thirty.)

When Treasurer Smith did give a report, it was always thorough and impressive. On the evening that Secretary McIntosh retired from his postmastership, Lobster Club, No. 1, held a special meeting to honor him, and Treasurer Smith's report was much appreciated. He expounded on the amazing growth of the postal service during Mr. McIntosh's term of office. Foreign mail, alone, had jumped from 125 to 658 (expressed in millions) and the deficit greatly extended. Lobster Club, No. 1, had cushioned the deficit each year, and with modest interest applied Mr. McIntosh now owed the Lobster Club, No. 1, the amount shown on the bill now rendered, which Mr. Smith presented to Mr. McIntosh. It was a poignant moment, and Member Noyes Lawrence moved that the bill be received with thanks, marked paid, and placed in the archives. Mr. Lawrence also took that opportunity to inform the membership that the meeting planned for next month at the Seaside Tearoom at Harpswell Point had been cancelled. He said the two nice little ladies that operated the Seaside Tearoom had died of food poisoning.

Secretary McIntosh responded with a forty-five-minute speech, reading from notes on a two-cent postage stamp.

On that evening when Reggie Bouchard spoke, President Stowe wrapped his gavel at last, and said, "All right, Boys, the fun is over—we'll now hear from our speaker, Reggie Bouchard!"

32 Bingo! For Steel Ceilings

Something else lost to the State of Maine as improvements accrued is the fun of looking in windows. Years ago, now, Joe Toth looked across his lawn at the home of Chet Wallace, and he could see Chet sitting at his kitchen table eating his breakfast. As Joe looked, Chet reached over and pushed a slice of bread into his electric toaster. So Joe waited just long enough for the slice of bread to reach the light brown stage and he rang Chet's number on the telephone. Joe saw Chet react when his

telephone rang, and then Chet got up and walked over to answer
it. When Chet said hello, Joe engaged him in small talk for a
moment, and then said, "Chet, what's that I smell burning there
at your place?"

Chet said, "Migod! My toast!" Then Joe saw Chet raising the
kitchen window to air the place out. So looking in windows can
be fun, and I found it fun for a good many years—until television came along and ruined this simple pleasure. Today, nothing much seems to take place in the windows of Maine. You can
drive around after dark, and all you see in a window is the bluish
glow of the picture tube, and Plato's captives staring at the shadows until they believe they are real.

I'm not talking about peeping. Peeping is a sneak thing, done
on purpose at close range, and not always for proper reasons.
I'm talking about the fleeting idylls and tableaux of family living
as seen from the roadway. People used to do things in their
kitchens and living rooms, and even bedrooms, so a ride through
the countryside was a cameo sequence—brief visits one by one
with the families along the way. I remember the head and shoulders of a grandmotherly sort, and just as we drove by she lifted
a sock she'd been darning on a darning ball and bit off the yarn.
That one was done! For a mile or more my wife and I talked
about the things used in times past for darning balls. A gourd,
a turkey egg, and the patent kind with a handle bought in a
store. Some women just shoved in a hand and spread the fingers to stretch the sock.

Maybe once in a while there'd be a sight worth slowing down
for. There was a man stripped to the waist (well, to the windowsill) and a doctor going over his lungs with a stethoscope.
Remember *house calls?* We hoped the gentleman was just having
a slight cold. We didn't linger on that one, but we did when we
saw the man whetting a knife. This man had a butcher knife and
was snickering it on a steel. On the table before him lay a supply
of venison, skinned out but the antlers still in place. Since this
was in August, we surmised poaching, but such is the Maine
attitude that the gentleman hadn't bothered to pull a shade. Before

we moved along he had made a good start on his freezer's supply of "lamb."

I always liked to see the wallpaper. Bedroom papers run to rosebuds, or some kind of flower, and my wife would say, "Oh! I like that one!" And we used to shout Bingo! at tin ceilings. I never knew much about them and wondered. There must be an academic study in tin ceilings, the rise and fall of. They were usually called "steel" ceilings, and a householder would have a room "steeled." In the town of Union there's a church with the auditorium "steeled" in somebody's memory. That's what the little plaque says. Some company somewhere must have made the steel panels with their patterns, and the salesmen who came around must have been persuasive. There must have been crews that came around to install, and if the ceilings were sold on time a collector of payments due. My window looking, while it was still something to do, suggested that any late 19th Century home will have at least one tin ceiling.

And we noticed that a room with a tin ceiling would likely be furnished in keeping. A parlor, or foot-pump, organ was a safe bet, along with whatnots and a marble-topped stand—more than a few marble-topped stands would have an Edison phonograph with the morning-glory horn. If not, then the family Bible. Corner hutches, and souvenir plates hanging on the walls. And when we saw people, they were always doing something, such as the Grammie darning socks. Children would be at the kitchen table doing school work. Once we saw some young folks pulling taffy. Another time two boys were carving jack-o-lanterns. And there was one boy gesticulating dramatically before a long mirror—I knew what he was about! He was practicing for a speaking contest. Memorize the words, and then do your gestures before a mirror. O Cataline, how long must we endure your unbridled audacities? And ever so many times we'd see two heads bent over a checker board—or a couple of enemies settling the world's cribbage championship again.

It was interesting to notice the illumination. At first, out in the country, everybody had plain, old-time kerosene lamps that gave a yellow glow, and with one lamp on the kitchen table every-body in the family sat close by—Mother knitting, Father reading the paper, and the children doing homework. One such tableau had everybody picking over dry beans—or we presumed that was the chore since our family used to do that, too. But as time passed the yellow light of a kerosene lamp would give way to the whiter light of the Reo. The Reo was a refinement, but not so much so as the Aladdin, which came later and had a mantle. The Aladdin gave a brighter white light, and a window aglow with an Aladdin could be spotted far down the road. Families that used to huddle in a kerosene glow now sat farther apart. Then as power lines were extended the electric lamp prevailed, and anybody passing could see everything much better.

But all that is gone. Today, the prevailing light in a roadside window is the pale, greenish blue of the television screen—the distorted spectrum of the one-eyed monster that has the popu-lace in thrall. It's been a long, long time since I've seen anything in a window along the road that is worth looking at. I might as well stay home and look at TV. One evening not long ago we found a barn with that pale, greenish blue light of the TV in the tie-up windows. The farmer had a television set, and all the cows were staring at it.

33 Some Corner of a Foreign Field

Now that a man can step inside a tin can and buzz off to see what the Planet Neptune looks like from the back-side, the red Lancastrian rose that blooms each July by my doorstep has a message. We call this Aunt Eunice's Rose, and for no more than a week once a year it gives us tiny, fragrant buds for the breakfast table to remind us of a little lady who came to Maine "from away" but didn't want to. Today, folks "from away" somewhat dominate the Maine scene and we have various names for them which are not always kindly. They boil up our Maine Turnpike and at the first gasoline pump they like to say that gasoline is cheaper back home. Roots today are not so important. Aunt Eunice came from England, which was more than a breakfast time away, and America was simply beyond her comprehension. She didn't want to be a settler and she didn't want to be a pioneer. But adversity had complicated her situation, and there came the suggestion that she leave her cottage in Lancashire and make the move to a new land. She was assured that the Indians had cooled down a good bit of late, and days went by when nobody had to roust a bear out of the kitchen. Comforts, she was told, had advanced so that people in America even had chairs. At that time Aunt Eunice was forty years old, unmarried, and it was the year 1792. She was also bereft and penniless, alone in her beloved England.

My great-great-grandmother, who was niece to Aunt Eunice, was then but nineteen, had three children, and was living comfortably in a log cabin of one room, with a loft, surrounded by the Maine wilderness, which had both Indians and bears. She could chop down a tree as well as her husband could, and worked with him as they cleared land. She paid little attention to the bears. But she couldn't write, so she walked ten miles to have Squire Bibber pen the letter that invited Aunt Eunice to come to America, to "The Maine," and start a new life. The log cabin was to be replaced by the first frame dwelling in the township, and by the time Aunt Eunice arrived a room of her own would be ready. Destitute, Aunt Eunice really had no choice.

Coming to Maine at that time was by no means as difficult as our schoolbooks sometimes make out. The people who were already here were doing well with fishing and farming, and several hundred vessels were making voyages back and forth to

England with salt cod, lumber, and even some manufactured products. The letter to Aunt Eunice, and her reply, took no great time. There had been a mite of fuss over sending money for passage to Aunt Eunice—the "colonies" were now a new nation, and dollars and cents hadn't yet achieved esteem in Britain. But arrangements were made and Aunt Eunice made ready with trepidation, and no great desire. She sailed, and amongst her very brief effects she had a potted red Lancashire rose in good British soil—there was going to be one corner of a foreign field that would be forever England.

People who think nothing of jetting afar and then coming home can't be expected to appreciate Aunt Eunice's abhorrence of the voyage. Nor was she about to adjust easily to her new home when she got here. True, the brand new "shingle palace" was far better in every way than her little cottage had been beside the Ribble River, and her windows looked on some fine scenery. And she was to have every loving care with kindness and comfort. But she kept up, all her life, a running innuendo that she was not happy and missed her real home. She never became an American, and—worse still—she never became a Mainer. She didn't make any complaints, mind you, but she was grudging with praise. The one indelible memory our family has kept alive is her vigilance in attending her bloomin' rosebush, and her unyielding insistence that without it the New World would be intolerable. She had planted it by the front steps of the new house within minutes of her arrival, and there it was to bloom forever—at least it has until now.

Aunt Eunice helped with the house and farm, minded the babies, and became a family establishment into the third generation. She spun, she knitted, she wove. She cooked, and she was "nasty-neat" about the house until the men would go and sit in the barn. She was an influence for rectitude, piety, and culture. There was no school, no church, and no near neighbors, so Aunt Eunice taught the rudiments, insisted on thanks and please, and expounded the Scripture. She also taught Great-great-grandmother to read and write—although there were interruptions with babies and chopping trees, if not with bears. Oh, yes—there was a Wawenok Indian sachem named Peter with whom Great-great-grandfather was friendly, and whenever Peter came to call and break bread Aunt Eunice would stay in her room.

So, you see, there was Aunt Eunice, transplanted unwillingly into our rough, uncouth wilderness, into a home that was never to be wholly hers. She never had "chick nor child" of her own, but she has remained through the generations far better remembered than those who did. We still bake her cookies, make her pickles, and wear her double-knit fox-and-geese mittens. And every summer, as June lingers into July, Aunt Eunice's Lancaster roses bloom by the front door and she has her long life beyond life. Every year as I gather the first full bud for our breakfast table I take the time to say, "Thank you, Aunt Eunice!"

34 The Thumb Is in Style

The age of Miss Martha Bragdon is nothing you can wring from me, but we were in school together and you can make a guess after hearing what she said. I stop to visit with her when I go that way, and as we sat on her front porch an automobile stopped in the road to pick up a hitchhiker. Miss Bragdon said, "You know—running boards were a great thing!" I followed her train of thought and agreed—thanking her for reminding me. In her time, and mine, giving a youngster a ride to the village was hardly the involved exercise we had just watched from her porch. The automobile stopped, the driver reached to open the door, the boy got in, the driver told him to fasten his seat belt, the door was closed, and the automobile moved along.

Automotive design has become complicated, and custom has wrought dubious improvements. It never occurred to that boy that he could walk to the village in five minutes, but would wait ten for a ride. Now that a ride had appeared, getting into the seat was a task. And at the post office, the boy had to get out again. All because the running board is extinct. In the days of running boards—the days of Miss Bragdon and me—if somebody offered us a ride there was no need to stop. The driver, not to be warned against hitchhikers for at least ten years, would see somebody walking up ahead and would tootle softly on his squeeze bulb, or push the button on his klaxon, signifying a willingness to cooperate, and the walker would prepare to do so. Vehicular speed, never more than 25 mph, would be reduced to 6 or 7, and the walker would hop onto the running board and hang on all the way to town. Nobody had to open any doors. Seat belts hadn't entered anybody's mind, and at the speeds of those days would seem to have no future. An affable motorist, himself going for his mail, would arrive at the post office with several people hanging on both sides, a pleasant way to arrive. The mortality statistics of highway travel had not yet rivalled the casualties of wars and acts of God. Highway safety, Miss Bragdon and I can testify, was not then something to worry about.

After the automobile picked up the hitchhiker, Miss Bragdon and I chatted, and I told her about the time five of us boys had been disporting in Estes Brook on a sweet August afternoon, and while walking home we had been invited to use the running boards on the beautiful Saxon owned, and driven, by Mr. Lemuel Franks. The Saxon was a sporty car, but lacked power, and when we five boys hopped on the running boards the motor ceased. Having just left the brook, we were about halfway up the Blackstone rise when Mr. Franks came along. So we hopped off again, pushed the Saxon up the rise, and jumped on again when the Saxon began going down hill. Whether Mr. Franks had neglected to check his brake rods, or the weight of five well-fed boys affected the kinetics I do not know, but the Saxon gathered speed on the down-grade and was tooling right along when Mr. Franks tried to slow. We enjoyed the wildest ride ever offered by a Saxon, and bounced into Asa Monroe's front field, right in a row of Blue Hubbard squashes, quite a step from the road.

Miss Bragdon asseverated rightly that such an incident today would fetch the police, ambulances, renewed recitations of the highway safety slogans, and while Mr. Monroe sued Mr. Franks over the damaged squashes, all our parents would sue Mr. Franks for whiplash. But those were running-board days, and we just tipped the Saxon back on its wheels (Mr. Monroe helped us) and pushed it to the road. When we pushed it fast enough so the engine "caught," we hopped on and Mr. Franks took us to town. As I recall, Mr. Franks thanked us. And we, of course, thanked him. Miss Bragdon said she remembered the Saxon automobile, and remembered that of Mr. Franks in particular, and she said if anybody drove a Saxon he was smart to pick up all the help he could get.

Hopping on running boards was no more than an extension of hopping sleigh runners. During the early years of automobiles in Maine it was customary to put them "up for the winter." Blocks of wood under the axles, so the tires were off the floor, and everything rested until the mud dried out in the spring. But sleighs still existed, and even the few folks who had a "car" kept a horse for snow season. If any nut in those days had suggested plowing snow off a highway he'd have had his come-uppance quickly. Snow was for sleddin' and sleighin'. The runners on a sleigh, and pung, extended backwards beyond the seat, so a boy wanting a ride could jump on, hands on the back of the seat and one foot on the runner. This was "hooking" a ride. A sleigh runner lacked the security of a running board, because a foot could, and did, get brushed off. The runner had no freeboard. I remember vividly how extensive a period of time elapsed after a foot got brushed off and I hit the snowbank. And how I'd walk back looking in the snow for my schoolbooks, my lunch pail, and the handful of papers with A's on them that proved how smart I was.

Not all the farmers did, but some would slow the horse while we got on (two of us—one on each runner) and then would say, "Are you all set?"

"Eyah."

"Then hang on!" and Ol' Fan would get touched up and think she was back on Topsham Track doing ha'f-past-two again. If a foot slipped, the rider was in the snowbank, but if he could hang on the ride was one for the Smithsonian. After a bit the farmer would rein in and say, "There—how's that?" if anybody was there to hear him. I say "farmer," but in truth the farmers usually had pungs rather than sleighs—the pung was a box sleigh built closer to the road, less stylish. The sleigh was stylish, but not as much as the cutter. We had only one cutter in our town—driven by the banker and he didn't permit free rides.

So we came to know when we could hook a ride and when we shouldn't, and we understood we mustn't jump on the sleigh of the Rural Free Delivery mailman. Authorized riders only; rules and regulations of the postal service. I'm positive those who "liked children" were more numerous then, and many a horse was reined to a stop, if there was room in the seat, for somebody—anybody—to get in. It was great to fit in under the comfort of the "buffalo robe." Probably any of us boys, and Miss Bragdon, too, in her time, could have outrun any nag in town, but there was a dashing illusion about having the snow brush your foot, and always the hope it wouldn't get brushed off. I never did get brushed off any running boards.

Miss Bragdon said she supposed a good part of the old-time fun came from knowing everybody. And everybody knew us. Those were days of short rides and few strangers. When sleighs went their way, and then when running boards ceased to be, the uplifted thumb came into style. Miss Bragdon said, "My, yes—Oh, Dear!"

35 Elegance Goes with 4-H Pigs

Not long ago one of these wondrous products of the New Culture called me on the telephone to say he would like to talk with me, as he had a desire to pursue literature and become a writer. Thinking perhaps I could persuade him to become a plumber, or something useful, I readily agreed to give him some time. When he came I listened in awe as he told me everything I needed to hear. Awe, because he was facile in his discourse to an extent I hadn't expected. And I had respect, too, because at his age I was hardly articulate and had a way of keeping things to myself. This lad was certainly away ahead of me, and as he pursued his plans to change the tides and alter the course of the sun, I wondered if he had the faintest idea how to get a hog into a crate. This is hardly an idle thought. It would be revealing, I'm sure, if a survey could be made of modern youth to ascertain how many gifted young students, eager for reform and willing to share, can make a pig do something a pig doesn't want to do.

Last fall, for the first time in many years, I went to a fair. Our fairs used to be great fun, and instructive. But the old agricultural exhibitions didn't last beyond their own time and the word "fair" hardly applies today. When the Maine legislature legalized parimutuel betting, the doom of our country fairs was sealed. All at once the emphasis was on the race track and while every fair modernized by erecting new bleachers, the old twenty-five cent prize for the biggest pumpkin, first offered in 1823, remained into the new age and attracted few pumpkins. Farming and homemaking no longer interested the association trustees, and the longest trace of corn or the prettiest quilt had little to do with bringing in the crowd. In my boyhood, everybody went to the fairs—my favorite was Topsham Fair—and all at once I didn't go to a fair.

But this last fall, hearing that Blue Hill Fair still operated without gambling at hoss-trots, I went to Blue Hill Fair. Even though it was more an exercise in memory, I did recapture some of the old-time enthusiasm. I had a sweet cider with a Ladies' Aid doughnut, and even a pink spun sugar. And I stayed on the last day after the crowd had left to see the animals taken from the exhibition pens to be returned to their farms. I watched the 4-H Club boys trying to crate their baby pigs. It was a shame the crowd had left, because here was the best show of the whole fair. It should have been done before the bandstand, marked "SPECIAL" in the printed programs. The shouting, squealing, chasing, escaping, and tumbling hullabaloo went on and on, and not one of the dozen or so boys had the slightest influence on his shoat. Not a pig was being caged. Each exhibition pen had a pull-up gate, against which the cage was pushed to receive, and once the boy got his pig through the opening the gate could be pushed down. A pig is not by nature cooperative in this simple exercise.

How often, in human affairs, do right-thinking people direct themselves with zeal and purpose towards utter failure! How often does the pig, fanciful or fact, just when success is assured, dart nimbly betwixt somebody's legs and thwart the best intentions! Here, in essence, is the Great Crusade, of noble purpose and laudable intent, frustrated by a grim fact of life. All the tumult and the shouting, all the labor and all the fuss, and all for naught! So far not one baby pig was ready to leave Blue Hill Fair.

Without any question, those 4-H boys know ever so much more about farming than I ever did. When each selected the pig as his project, he immediately received books and pamphlets and bulletins telling him every known fact about pigs and their requirements. Porcine management in its entirety right down to the last squeal. The Extension Service has specialists and experts on call to answer any question. Back when I had a pig, we were still going by Vergil's *Eclogues.* I didn't know a roughage from a concentrate, and we still called garbage *swill.* I used to go and slop my pig, whereas these Blue Hill boys administer nutriments. There is an elegance goes with today's 4-H pigs, but behind that elegance lurks an unchanged fact—the pig hasn't changed one bit. His intellectual patterns remain unaltered and he gives no attention whatever to what the professors have been doing at the universities. But when I was a 4-H lad, I knew how to crate a hog.

I sense a large and significant moral is approaching.

I was not wearing my blue suit at Blue Hill Fair. By blue suit, I mean my farmer's dungarees and work shirt. Haberdashery for agronomical purposes. I was sporting that day, so had on my "other ones" and a necktie. For any kind of a pig caper I was in sartorial nicety. But I gladly sacrificed my splendor that day, and in the urgency of teaching a new generation an old trick, I jumped a fence into a pen. The squealing pig had just knocked his juvenile owner galley-west, tail over bandbox. The boy gave me a dirty look, which may have been meant for the pig, and I clapped a pail over the pig's snout. I thus had, you might say, a pig in a pail. People could see that I had a pig in a pail, and by that time I was playing to a considerable array of spectators—friends and relatives of the 4-H boys, and odd ones attracted by the hubbub. I then deftly manipulated the pail so in attempting to back out of it the baby pig backed himself through the gate and into his cage. The pig, be-pailed, was silent and the maneuver took all of five seconds. I then passed the pail to the boy in the next pen, and one by one the pigs were ready to ride home. No chasing, no squealing, no errors.

I learned that from my grandfather, who was an eminent authority on pig psychology. One day long before I was 4-H age he had a load of hogs going to the Brighton abattoir, and he'd tied some long boards inside his hayrack to make a travel cage for them. He had a plank for a ramp, and using a pail, he had backed each hog up the plank and into the rack. No fuss. Gramp hadn't worked up a sweat, and the hogs hadn't been chased and frightened. Completely relaxed, the animals set out happily for Brighton. At the team track in the village, he got the pigs into a box car the same way.

I did have to brush my shoes and shine them again when I got home from Blue Hill Fair, but I was pleasantly smug about my know-how at handling pigs. I thought about that day as I talked to this young man who sought my advice about becoming a writer. I think he knew a good deal more right then than I ever shall.

36 Bent Over like an Old Man

The first time I became aware of this new-day deference to the old folks was at the bowling alley. The young dream who handles the cash register asked me my age. I'm not sensitive about that and was about to tell her when something nudged me not to. Why was she asking that? I had come in to whoop it up with the boys—my usual Wednesday evening outing as lead-off athlete for our town-league team, the Ridge Runners. Would it be possible that this sweet young thing had been noticing me secretly, admiring something about me, and curious about my being old enough? Had my smooth prowess on the candlepin alley impressed her until she felt I was well preserved? So I held back on telling her my age, and I said, "So you noticed?"

She backed off at that and said, "Well, the old folks get senior-citizen rates." At that moment I became a senior citizen.

The new philosophies have intruded often since then, and I get asked to subscribe to the retired persons' magazines, but I find myself resisting. I have been something of a resister anyway. I frequently shun the zip code. I have punched holes in computer cards. I do not have an all-purpose charge card, useful in 427 countries at three million shops. Some days I buy things and pay cash, taking my 2 percent. I always write something where it says do not write in this space. And as I moseyed along feeling fit I supposed that senior citizens are old mossbacks who sit around discussing William McKinley and listening to their arteries harden. Now I am jerked up short by a pretty girl who wants to know my age. It was disconcerting to learn I'm entitled to low rates at the bowling alley. This pretty girl seemed to think I had attained honor and merit by being over the hump. Saving a few cents at the cost of being aged doesn't appeal to me. I didn't, and I don't, feel that way about it. I didn't enjoy having senility shoved down my throat when I was, so to speak, at the very peak of my talents. I still bowl a perky 84, and I did that when I was in my thirties.

I have not lived in a context and a tradition that looks upon age as a milestone or a goal. There was never a time, as I recollect, when a person should be told, "Now you are old!" That began with compulsory retirement notions, and with the magic dates of the Social Security System. Good old Uncle Sam started the "Now-you-are-old" business. When I hit sixty-five I got a card telling me to go to Social Security and "secure my benefits." I did go, and the woman's first question was, "Now, when did you retire?"

I said, "From what?"

When my grandfather was eighty-four he fell out of an apple tree. It was a Tolman Sweet tree, just below the barn, and over the years the cattle had reached up to prune it, so the tree stood tall. Gramp was up on the twenty-five-foot ladder, and there were no lower limbs to support it. When Gramp came down, he came down all the way, basket and all, and he landed a-slant on a beehive. This broke three ribs and bruised the apples. In telling about this, Gramp said it inconvenienced him some. He said, "It hurt! It hurt like the very devil! Why, I was walking around all bent over like an old man."

It was that same fall, not long after the tumble, that a meat peddler from the city came down to see if Gramp would sell the three-year-old steer he had in the pasture. It was a good time to sell, because as soon as it snowed Gramp would have to feed the animal in the barn. So the meat man paid for the steer and Gramp folded the money in his pocket. Gramp said, "You wait here, and I'll go drive the steer down from the pasture."

I happened to arrive just then, one of my occasional visits to see how Gramp was making out, and here was this strapping man sitting on the steps while my poor, aging grandfather was running around up in the pasture.

When my Aunt Grace married Bert Moore, Grandfather walked to town and took the steam cars to go and see what his new son-in-law looked like. Gramp had to get a neighbor to come and do the chores. Gramp found his new son-in-law a right-enough chap, and they hit it off fine. Uncle Bert suggested they walk around and see his place. He reached in a hall rack and picked out a walking stick, a cane. He handed it to Gramp. Gramp swished it around and thought that was dandy. Then he looked at Uncle Bert, and he said, "Where's your stick?"

"Oh," said Bert, "I don't need one."

This snide suggestion that my grandfather was elderly hurt his feelings, and he tossed the walking stick back on the porch and proceeded to walk Uncle Bert's legs off. Uncle Bert, at the time, was twenty-three.

Or, take Cousin Jimmy. Jimmy Edgecomb. He lived on Federalist Ridge up at Industry, and the family gathered one day to help him celebrate his hundredth birthday anniversary. Tables were set on the lawn, under an apple tree, and Cousin Jimmy got the full treatment. But that morning, just before sun-up, Cousin Jimmy had been roused by the squealing of his pig. He pulled his pants on over his nightshirt, grabbed a "Queen's Arm" musket behind the kitchen door, and rushed to the barnyard to shoot a black bear that was giving his pig a hard time. The birthday party decor was rounded out by the bear—it was dressed out and hanging on the apple tree limb, not far from the birthday cake and the punch bowl. Everybody took pictures of Cousin Jimmy standing beside the bear. A man, they say, is as old as he feels.

Away back in the beginnings we had an ancestor who got fired up with patriotism, and he decided to go to Louisbourg with Pepperrell and do what he could. Everybody tried to dissuade him, mostly because of his age, which was seventy-eight. He said he was in the prime of life and would be a big help. He'd made up his mind, and no use to protest—he was going. On the morning he left, his father came down and said he was going to go with him. He said the boy was too young to go alone and needed somebody to take care of him. Things worked out very well, because the boy was wounded in the fighting, and without his father to take care of him he might not have come home at all. And, I wouldn't be here today.

Then there's another way to look at it. When little Buster Leavitt was five years old his mother enrolled him in the summer playground activity. This was all brand new at that time, and the recreational program was considered a big advancement. But Buster came home after the first session and said he wasn't going again. He said, "I don't get any fun out of winding maypoles with a bunch of kids."

I just don't agree that there's a magic click in some kind of a golden wheel that tells when bowling prices go down for the old duffers. I don't agree that there is a set date when a citizen turns senior and should relax. I don't want to save ten cents a string because I'm senile any more than I want somebody helping me in and out of my bowling shoes. The generation gap is no wider from my side than it is from yours. I told the cash-register girl I'd let her know.

37 Fred Was in Good Health

The great clamor augments and persists—we unfortunate bumpkins out here in the country are told that our salvation depends on the welfare of the cities. The mayors of New York dwell in succession on this theme and all the other mayors yelp at their heels like a cry of coon-hounds in a sweet corn patch. If we don't save the cities, all will be lost. We country people, trying to make out, weep like anything and resolve more and more to do what we can. I'm sending a CARE package to the present mayor of New York City, who has four tuxedos but is destitute.

Some of the evidence belies this clamor. One of my pastoral amusements is to tune in Radio WEEI in Boston, which reaches the Maine Coast nicely, and listen to the skyway patrol that scans the traffic situation. The "eye-in-the-sky" boy describes affairs on Storrow Drive, the Tobin Bridge, and tells how things go on Route 128, and this is supposed to help folks who are driving to work. This is a boon to the cosmopolite. The boy up in the helicopter effects a voice of high excitement, so he sounds like somebody about to jump off the roof before the building blows up. All this may be of great importance in Boston, but here at down-Maine Friendship I am amused. Nobody tells me if there is much traffic between Friendship and Cushing, or between Cushing and Friendship, so I am able to concentrate on Storrow Drive and the Tobin Bridge. One morning there was an eleven-car crash on Morrissey Boulevard, but we've never been lucky enough to have one of *those* on the Salt Pond Road.

But we may, yet. Well, these Boston highway pilots used to work Monday to Friday, and because Saturday and Sunday are not commuter days they'd sleep in. But last summer they began "monitoring" the vacation routes, and as city people left for the mountains, the lakes, and the sea, WEEI began giving traffic conditions on the roads to Cape Cod, to the White Mountains, and the Maine Turnpike. Everybody in the magnificent city, it seems, is getting to hell out to squander the weekends amongst the rigors of country life. Saturdays and Sundays are now more frantic than Mon–Fri. Nobody wants to stay in the cities. So as the mayors clamor to save the cities, we seem to have something in a sling.

If I'm going to be obliged to pay taxes to help the cities, I want to insist that city people stay home to enjoy my philanthropy. Let 'em go and ram around in the Callahan Tunnel. Why should I, and my bucolic friends, subsidize an eleven-car smash-up on the Salt Pond Road?

Back when there seemed to be a presumption the Russians were going to drop atomic bombs on our cities, Boston had a big evacuation plan worked out. Everybody, after the bomb, would follow instructions on the radio, and direction signs along the way, and would come up to Maine, where we were supposed to be glad to see them and give them food, shelter, and loving care. I didn't hear that anybody in Boston came up to consult us about this mass salvation. I shuddered as I pondered on the arrival of this horde, and how long it would take it to empty my freezer. The thought is disturbing. But there was a smile. The society lady who headed up this post-bomb hegira deigned to grant an interview to the press, and she said all was in readiness for this mass evacuation. She, herself, had her own arrangements completed, and would join the inhabitants of Boston as they sought succor and safety. She had baskets for her two cats, and a month's supply of cat food. Casualties in the destruction of Boston would exceed a million people, but Maine would gain two cats.

While I have your attention, I'll tell about Fred Gilbert. Fred found out that Boston traffic offers no great problem. He didn't need a helicopter in the sky. Fred was a most interesting man. He made his home in Greenville, right where Moosehead Lake begins, and he was in Boston only once in his life. Fred pronounced his name gil-burt, but his cousins over in Beauce, Quebec, kept with the zheel-bare, wit' de h'ac-sent on de las' syl-LAB-b'l. There are many Gilberts in that country and most of them work in the woods. Fred harvested firewood. When the Great Northern was cutting an area, the pulpwood crew would leave the hardwood and Fred would follow to harvest it. Sometimes he'd have a small crew, but mostly he worked alone. You'd see his piles of yellow birch, maple, beech, and ash by the roadsides if you went into the area—waiting to be scaled and hauled down to Greenville. An outdoors man, Fred was strong and never had a sick day in his life.

But one day he came into the office of Doc Pritham and said he wasn't feeling up to snuff. Doc Pritham already has his competent biographer, so there's no need to dwell on him here. He looked Fred over and couldn't find anything essentially wrong. But Doc said, "Look, Fred—we don't grow any younger. I never looked you over before, so I have no medical record. So I'm going to make a date for you at the clinic down in Boston, and I want you to go and get the full treatment. They'll give you all the tests that I can't do, and they'll send me a report in about a week."

So Fred's alarm clock went off on a particular morning at two o'clock, and he descended long before Rosy-fingered Dawn had walked o'er the dew, and he got in his pick-up truck and started for Boston. About the time Boston was readying, Fred was well into Massachusetts, and he approached the city more in awe than in trepidation. He had never seen a city, except for St. Georges-Est in Kaybeck. This was before helicopters scanned the highways, and before radios in pick-up trucks. Fred had good directions for finding the clinic, and he was glad to find a place to park his pick-h'up, right under a tree. He went for his tests.

As Doc Pritham had said, he got the full treatment, and the doctors and nurses were delighted by his strangulated h'English. When he came back to his parked truck, he found it surrounded by a circle of Boston policemen—they were speculating among themselves as to what this might be, anyway. One of them was looking at the gasoline fire pump, and another had a peavey in his hand. The pick-up had, in addition, a lot of chain and rope, several hydraulic twenty-ton jacks, a skidder tire, some skidder cables, extra gasoline, two "shinesaw," and other things indigenous to the Maine woods—there is no law north of Greenville and no god beyond Seboomook. Fred was curious at this congregation and approached with a question—"Whassamatter, somet'ing is wrong?"

The policemen turned to look at Fred. "Who are you?"

"Fred Gilbert—dis my pick-h'up."

"You're from Maine?"

"Ah, oui—yes. Greenville, h'all de way."

"Well," said a policeman with a courtly bow, "it's a great pleasure to meet you. Now, it's against the law to park like this on Boston Common."

"Boston *what*?" asked Fred. "I'm not know dat."

"Get in," said an officer. "And drive off!"

They headed him toward Storrow Drive and said, "And keep on going!"

"Great pleasure for mak' some acquaintance," said Fred. "Bonjour! Au revoir!"

"Get to hell outa here!"

Fred miscued. With his good woodsman's sense of direction he backtracked out of Boston, and got on the wrong deck of the Tobin Bridge. He got as far as the toll booths before he got flagged down. Somebody decided wisely it would be easier to get Fred off the bridge in the direction he was headed than to turn him around. Accordingly a police cruiser came to convoy Fred northerly in the southbound traffic. "He ain't paid the toll," said the attendant.

"Damn the toll!" said the policeman, and he escorted Fred not only off the bridge, but all the way to Lynnfield. Then he got Fred on the Maine-bound lane and told him not to stop until he got beyond New Hampshire. "Goodbye," he said, "and I mean it!"

Fred said, "T'ank you ver' much!"

The policeman said, "Don't mention it."

It was after dark when Fred got to Greenville, and it had been a long day. The next morning he went to Scott Brook and resumed cutting firewood. A week later Doc Pritham got the reports, and there was nothing whatever the matter with Fred Gilbert.

"Except," Doc Pritham told him, "you don't want to forget you're seventy-nine years old."

38 First, Have a Boiled Dinner

As the days have passed and been replaced with others of a questionable nature, we should consider the brine barrel and the disintegration of the red-flannel hash philosophy. Every once in a while somebody from Maine who is "living short" in a far place will come home to visit, and the first thing he wants is a boiled dinner. But the real boiled dinner is getting harder and harder to find in Maine, and our chain-store markets have been foisting off "kosher" brisket for some time without any loud complaints. Even the clerks think that's corned beef. Corned beef does not look like a boiled lobster.

Historically, the Mainer's love for salt—corned—beef is a paradox. A people who went on long sea voyages to far places, or spent the winters in log-cabin lumber camps, well knew what salted meats were. After a few meals of unaltered sameness, the hanker for anything out of a brine wears off, and always at sea and mostly in lumber camps the brine barrel was constant. In Maine tradition, unprincipled chandlers and commissaries swindled off superannuated draft horses for long voyages and long winters, and got little protest from seamen in the Indian Ocean and choppers at Churchill Lake. The brine barrel aboard ship became known as "the harness cask," and folklore insisted that aboard the brig *Eliza Brown*, as she rounded the Horn, the seacook served a set of hames in brown gravy. Now we have a population that doesn't even know what a hame is. And 'twas well known in the lumber camps that if anybody yelled WHOA at table the crew couldn't swallow until the cook yelled GID-DYAP! Meat pulled from the harness cask was freshened in sweet water, and at sea this was not always done so thoroughly as in camp, where water was handy. The cook made salt hoss "quick," which means not quite tender, but almost. That it might also be palatable was the chance a seaman took when he signed articles. In the Maine woods, the salt barrel was assisted by fresh meat at times—each camp had a professional hunter who brought in venison, moose, caribou, sometimes bear if one chanced out of hibernation during snow season, and fish caught through the ice. But shortly the state made it illegal to serve "game" and most of the meat hunters became game wardens. I like to think the Mainer's long suffering from salt hoss made him particular and accounts for his insistence on GOOD corned beef when he tackles it at home. Our traditional "corn" is light, and the brisket is good quality. Interesting, too, that some Mainers like a smoked pork shoulder with their boiled dinners instead of corned beef—a taste that has no precedent at sea or in the forest. Pork was as taboo there as it was in the Biblical wilderness, and for the same reason. The absolute need for a brine barrel, as preface to a boiled dinner, passed with refrigeration—today a piece of fresh meat can be used with a handful of salt in the pot. But, some, includ-ing me, saith that is not quite the same. Here and there in Maine are still some happy communities where the grocer keeps his harness cask busy. It is, or should be, a rotating asset. My wife, if she doesn't corn our own brisket at home, will tell the grocer when she'll come in for corned beef and how long she'd like it corned. Put and take. He keeps track of each piece. We always get a "light" corn.

On board ship, where vegetables were scarce, the left-over corned beef was converted to "plum duff," which was usually served on Sunday and was considered a dessert. The beef was chopped, raisins added, and boiled in a pudding bag. Sliced, it was served with a sweet sauce, usually vanilla. At sea, raisins were plums.

But ashore, on the family table, the left-over corned beef, with the vegetables that made it a "dinner," was a joyous triumph. The boiled dinner itself, as first presented, started with the boiled beef on a generous platter, surrounded by sufficient carrots, onions, parsnips, potatoes, and beets cooked separately so they wouldn't color the others. And cabbage—a boiled dinner was, and is, known sometimes as "corned beef and cabbage." Mustard at least, and horseradish at best, is applied to the beef, and a touch of mustard and vinegar on the cabbage. Dry mustard brought to perfection with sharp cider vinegar, and true horseradish ground in vinegar, of course. That's about it, except that the best part of a boiled dinner comes later—a totally different consequence from the maritime plum duff.

Oh—I forgot to mention: Sometimes a suitably sized piece of salt pork is boiled along with the corned beef—not so much to be served at table but to give the cooking meat a piquancy and character. It does no harm.

Now—to Red-Flannel Hash: Put the left-over beef through a meat grinder, or chop it. Do the same with the left-over vegetables, and this time run the red beets right through with the others. Combine the beef and vegetables, mix well, and make into patties. Fry the patties in (preferably) bacon fat until they are crispy top and bottom, but moist and hot inside. As you lift each patty from the frypan to serve it, have a dropped egg ready to put on top. Dropped is Maine for poached. Each customer will take two or more, whichever comes first. And will ask what the poor people are eating. For a reason that, along with other things that are now obscure, was once obvious, the beety confection was called Red Flannel Hash. It went with living in Maine, but not so much so now.

39 Everybody Out for Croquet!

A note in the news told us the German government is going to make a pitch for "Holidays on the Farm." Back into the country! The note added that the success of this rural movement will depend on the German farmers' willingness to arrange suitable entertainment programs. The minister of tourism says city folks soon tire of just scenery, fresh air, indolence, and leisure, and after the third or fourth day the customer will need organized play and planned amusement.

Well, maybe. The idea should be given thought. Maine, a pioneer in entertaining folks "from away," had a generation or so of profitable tourism from the "summer boarder" and the like, and about all we offered the guests was fresh air, scenery, indolence and leisure. Some places had a croquet set on the front lawn, but it was never listed in the attractions as organized activity. Maine had all sorts of summer resorts in those days, from the modest farmhouse looking down on a lake to the sumptuous niceties of Poland Spring, Samoset, Rangeley Lake House, Squaw Mountain, Kineo. And Maine also had some mighty good small hotels that were open all the time and depended on salesmen in off-season—Eagle Hotel in Brunswick, the DeWitt in Lewiston, the Falmouth at Portland, the Lancy House at Pittsfield, the Blethen at Dover-Foxcroft, the Penobscot Exchange at Bangor, and the Huston House at Mattawamkeag, mentioning a few and skipping many. The summer crowd wasn't their special income, but they took 'em in, and every one of those places had a dining room nobody faulted. Nobody in Maine, then, had the faintest idea what a "motel" was going to be. And, we had dozens of "summer camps" which opened for spring fishing, gave July and August over to the "vacationist," returned to fishing in September, and then took care of the hunters until the season closed. The common assurance that "every hunter gets his deer" acknowledged the kindness of the camp choreboy who kept spare bucks hanging in the icehouse for the "sports" who didn't shoot their own. Thus a paying guest who didn't know how to load his rifle would go home happy.

It was even so.

The hotels and camps could be expensive, but a couple of weeks on a farm were reasonable—room and board, a lawn swing, and croquet if so inclined. Some came and stayed and went home and never touched a croquet mallet. Organized recreation? You could drive along any Maine country road and tell which farms took summercaters. And—pay attention here!—Maine hadn't launched any official state agency to go after this business, and we hadn't set up any bureaus to license lawn swings or tax croquet sets. No regulating inspectors came around to look at chamber mugs and set up requirements for window screens. The farmer's wife cooked and served, and if somebody gave her a tip it was hers. Follow me?

We hadn't even thought of a tax on rooms to rent.

We mustn't overlook those "requirements which have to be met." Almost all of our wilderness camps, many of our elegant resort hotels, and more than a few of our summer boarding homes quit because of, among other things, state-house stupidity, federal harassment, and overzealous inspectors who came to make trouble. Other things helped, and changing times had an effect—the "overnight guest" replaced the good folks who used to come and stay a month. And the Maine liquor laws! These wilderness camps, giving the guests lake and forest, mountains and streams, couldn't apply for a cocktail license until April, which you might suppose would give plenty of time to issue a license to serve drinks before the camp opened the first week in June. The first week in June, in the Maine woods, is not always seven perfect days. The eager angler patiently awaits "ice out" and then arrives. June is still clinky around the edges. Said angler forthwith dumps the snow out of a boat and seeks the elusive trout and the wily salmon. At evensong, he returns to camp with his nose congealed, and he would like to sit by the lobby fireplace and thaw with a toddy at hand. He is, understand, paying good money and expects to have a good time.

"Sorry," says the choreboy, or the waitress, or the guide, or the proprietor, "we can't serve a drink—our cocktail license hasn't come."

This is a cheerful tiding, you bet.

Meantime, the astute legislature has appropriated more funds to advertise the attractions and advantages of the State of Maine, and the tub-thumpers are hard at work. Understand, most of these wilderness resort camps were located in "unorganized territory," which means the townships where they operated have no local government. The business of applying for a liquor license in an unorganized township is done through the county commissioners. Levi Hodgson used to claim he was a county commissioner in Somerset County for seventeen years and didn't know it, which can give you an idea. The county commissioners, eventually, forward such applications to the state house. An oddity of the liquor law, back then, was that a license for a bar couldn't be issued until the establishment had been inspected and passed. So the state house would notify the county commissioners that an inspector would attend shortly. April is long gone, and thirsty June anglers abound. How do you inspect a bar that isn't open yet? Along about the middle of July a Maine wilderness camp would get the license it needed, and should have had, last June. Meantime, being choreboy at one of those camps was a good job. The choreboy, who often was a man in his late seventies or so, would keep a supply of whiskey and sundries hidden in the sawdust of the icehouse, and thirsty anglers found he was always cooperative. Mason Peters, for years choreboy at Camp Kumagin, told me his best week was $3,220, net. Which, if you please, was money the proprietor of the camp never saw. It didn't figure in his profit and loss.

Don't blame the state altogether. Uncle Sam decided one year that waitresses and other help who got any should declare their tips as income. Maybe this was all right, but Uncle Sam made the poor camp owner responsible for declaring such earnings. He, already sore about his liquor license, said the hell with it. For more than one wilderness camp, this foolishness about waitresses and their tips was the last straw.

Well, the best enticement for the old-time Maine summer vacation was the total assurance that nobody was going to blow any whistles, ring any bells, or schedule contests, tournaments, and field events. The summer guest became family, and lolled about in sweet content until it was time to eat and sleep.

There was one young fellow, not quite my age, who developed a curious custom of becoming a summertime buddy. I wouldn't see him all winter, and then in June he'd show up and share my pleasures. He'd come walking through the woods every morning to play with me, and many times my mother would invite him to have lunch. He wasn't all that much fun, and I think my mother thought his homelife was lacking and he needed company. When he didn't get invited and went home for lunch, he'd scoot right back after eating and stay until supper time. Come to find out, this lad's mother took a summer boarder who would sit in the lawn swing to get his money's worth, and he couldn't stand to have this kid around. So every pleasant day right after breakfast he'd give the lad ten cents to run over and play with me. When my mother found this out she wasn't really pleased, but she disliked the kid, too, and she thought the summer boarder was smart. When the summer boarder went back to Philadelphia, we wouldn't see the boy all winter.

The summer boarder business, as Germany may learn, was lucrative, whereas running a summer resort or a hotel had its problems. The farm had no staff and no overhead. The farm didn't offer anything the farm family didn't use, and could give a summer boarder what he needed without added expense. Every Maine housewife was a good cook, and every farm had everything to cook with. The cows were milking, the hens were laying, the garden was generous, and the guests could fetch their own trouts from the pasture brook. Scenery was free for the looking and ready to look at all day long. The boarders could hike out and hike back, and if they didn't hike they could sit on the porch hammock and watch for somebody to come along the road. Some boarders were bird watchers, and went about with the Audubon book and binoculars. When the Kodak appeared, there was great taking of pictures of everything. Luke Potter took boarders, and he had a billygoat that used to climb up on the woodpile, and he said the boarders took so many pictures of the damned goat that he would smile when he heard somebody coming. Then they'd snap Elmer with a string of trout, Uncle Harry with a basket of t'martoes, and many another idyllic moment to show friends back in the city. Another thing—lacking organized activity, the summer boarders liked to help with the farm work, and the Kodak snapshots would show Miss Larney on a rack of hay, Mr. Foley picking blueberries, and Mrs. Warnock picking up a basket of eggs. Great stuff to adorn a winter in Philadelphia. If he wanted to, the summer boarder could hitch old Dolly to the buggy and take the other boarders for a ride.

There was one woman who came for years to summer with the MacEachern family and she became an oddity. All she did was sleep. And eat. She'd get up in the morning and tuck away a hired man's breakfast, and then go to the porch hammock and snore. She'd have an E. D. E. N. Southworth novel, but she didn't read much and never got through the first chapter. She'd fall right off to sleep, and wake in time for the next meal. She'd be famished. She came back every summer for ten years and never missed a meal. She was good for ten dollars a week and always stayed three weeks. The only programming she got was an effort to keep the youngsters quiet around the dooryard.

So things have, indeed, changed. We can wonder what the farmers of Germany are expected to do to provide scheduled recreation for their guests. Here in Maine we neglected that, but I surmise that's not the reason we pretty much went out of the summer boarder business.

40 Molly Was a Red Cow

"And how far did you reach back for *that!*" she asked, and it took me a moment to realize what she meant by *that*. I had taken a pitcher of new-day, rarefacted, pasteurized, modicated, homogenized, emaciated milk from the refrigerator and had idly stirred it with a spoon before pouring a glass as obbligato to a bedtime molasses cookie. When I was a boy, milk had lumps in it.

So I was reaching back a good many years. Back before we quit the cow business. There came a time when the various governments didn't seem friendly and the constant attendance of inspectors was wearing out my tie-up doorsill. I didn't greet any of these milk inspectors with wild tumult and cheers, but they came anyway, and those I drove away came back. There was one real tangle that brought things to a head. Three ambitious youngsters working their way through cow college came and started to go into my barn. I tried to dissuade them with gentle remonstrance, and they drew up into a haughty hooraw and told me I didn't have anything to say about it. They were federal inspectors, they said, and they were going to test my cows. I had no choice. I told them to wipe behind their ears and to get-lost. They heard me, because I articulated so a Rhode Island Red rooster I kept turned his head aside and blushed. Upon the insistence of this trio, still saying I had no right to keep them out of my barn, I said, "Show me a warrant, or something, that deprives me and supports you."

One of the boys opened a wallet and showed me a State of Maine automobile driver's license.

I quote myself exactly. I said, "If you think that is a ticket into my cow barn, you had best enter in a speedy manner, because right behind you and coming on fast will be a charge of double-B shot out of a ten-gauge fowling piece."

I added, "Shove off!"

One of the boys said, "You'll be involved with the best lawyers in Washington."

I replied, jocularly, "Maybe so, but you'll find lawyers are not always the best authorities on picking out bird shot."

They went away, promising to return. They didn't come back, because I stepped into the house and made a telephone call to our commissioner of agriculture at the state house, and I tingled his tympana some old goo-ood. He was Carl Smith, and he said not to fuss so, that this was a government project to help deserving boys earn college money, and it didn't cost the state a cent.

I never went into my own cow barn without first disinfecting my boots. I had a pan and a jug of magoozlum for that purpose by the door. These boys had been in and out of every tie-up in the county, and were going to walk into mine with every boogie they'd found intact and ready. What they were about to test for I never learned, but the confrontation was typical of the way dairy farmers were manhandled during those years when dairy farmers were being manhandled.

There were inspectors, some, who did have papers and possibly proper purposes. One day two inspectors came, and they said I'd have to put a peg in the wall so I could hang up my milking stool, and with them were two men in a limousine who said they were inspecting the inspectors. It was unhygienic to leave a milkstool on the floor when not in use. Since I had a few cows for family use only, and never sold any milk or butter, I sold my cows after the persecution began to get sticky, and we've bought milk at the stores ever since. There has been, thus, nothing in my milk pitchers that needed stirring since the days of Molly, who flourished about the time h-o-m-o-g-e-n-i-z-e got into the dictionary. And when the dictionary tells you what homogenize means, the dictionary is a cock-eyed liar.

Molly was a red cow, of a persuasion known as Durham, or Milking Shorthorn. The breed makes a good family cow, and has a retrieval value at the abattoir. They are not famous for "holding up" as the year runs along, but freshen liberally and then taper off. The quality of Red Durham milk is good, scoring maybe halfway between Jersey and Holstein. Jerseys have a high cream line, Holsteins don't. My grandfather used to explain that you could tell Jersey milk from Holstein milk by putting a dime in the milkpail. He said if the milk was creamy and just covered the dime—that was Jersey milk. But if the cow filled the pail to the brim and you could still see the dime, that was a Holstein. Molly, after she freshened, would be about halfway. After milk, butter, cream, and cottage cheese, Molly's surplus went into the slop barrel to feed the pigs or to nurture a veal lately disconnected from the parent stem. So her bounty went on and on. Molly was a pet. During Molly's time the only other milch cow we kept was a scrub Holstein that stood in during Molly's annual *arida nutrix* condition. The children were unhappy with that Holstein's blue milk and were glad when Molly had her calf and could join us again.

The manner in which we handled Molly's lacteal bounty is today as illegal as high treason. The pail, after milking (by hand), was brought to the house and the still warm milk was passed through a gauze filter—the only "processing" it got. Since our milk was used before the lactic enzymes could take over, there was no reason to pasteurize—and that's all pasteurization is for or ever was for. We had two crockery pitchers, alike, which held a half gallon each. One was filled after morning milking and the other at vespers. This was more milk than we used, so if it came time to refill a pitcher and it still had milk, we dumped the milk into the pig's bucket and started again. Then we had setting pans, flat tinware in which milk was put aside to "rise." We didn't have a separator. When the cream had risen, it was skimmed off, put in a crock, and later churned. We'd churn twice a week. The kind of cream we lifted for butter making is not seen today, anywhere, and was thicker than the same cream would be if separated by machine. It gained by waiting a spell, whereas a separator does its work on freshly drawn milk. The bacteria count in our butter cream would make a gong play like a carillon, and was far above the most tolerant figure allowed today by law. But that was what made it good. You see, without natural milk bacteria, milk won't sour, and when you kill off those bacteria, a kind of putrefaction sets in which is sold to the deceived public as "just as good as." Putrefaction is lawful, but real sour milk isn't. If cream such as we "skimmed" were to appear today anywhere in the United States on a cut of hot Red Astrachan apple pie, the entire staff of Health & Welfare in Washington would go into apoplexy. For that matter—probably the entire Department of Agriculture would mobilize and ask where anybody found some Red Astrachan apples.

Isn't it interesting that the foregoing lucid paragraph says so many things that nobody knows—and which nobody is going to believe? So the milk we put in the ice chest (refrigerators came later) would flex its muscles and perform as milk is supposed to, and the cream would rise and enthusiasm would accrue. Just as the churning cream "rose" in the pans, the cream would come to the top of the milk in our pitchers, so our breakfast cereal supply would have this wonderful, magnificent, yellow, rich scum, beautiful to behold. Pushing a long-handled spoon into it, the first user thereof would stir rapidly, mingling the scum back where it came from. The day began, you might say, when the milk got stirred for breakfast.

We always had porridge. Didn't everybody? So the first word spoken might be when a child got his bowl of porridge and then looked into the pitcher. "Mom! Did you stir yet?"

Mom would say, "All stirred!"

If a pitcher of milk hadn't been standing too long and the cream hadn't formed too strong a scum, mixing could be done by pouring a glass of milk and then dumping it back in the pitcher. Same effect, but with Molly's good cream it usually took a spoon to break through. Sometimes a smart-aleck youngster would lift out a good snatch of Molly's rich cream before he stirred, thus getting all-cream on his oatmeal—but leaving pretty much all skimmed-milk for the siblings. This was considered a naughty thing to do. And none of us would have believed the day would come when skim milk would appear in the stores—or that anybody in his right mind would buy it. Ah, yes! The Dairy Industry with its lackeys and its inspectors has put good, healthy, delicious, rich, yellow Molly-cream out of business and has removed it forever from the ingredients of human happiness.

So I absentmindedly turned the years back and stirred today's homogenized delicacy, which has no cream line and probably very little cream. Not so any cow would be pleased. I concluded that if a pitcher of honest milk should appear in the United States today, people would think it had something the matter with it. No lumps! I put the spoon down when she asked me, and I said, "Quite a few years!"

41 The Disasters Were Fun, Too

A gentleman who manufactures snowmobiles has advised me not to fight them—they are here to stay. Probably, but every snowmobile has to be driven by somebody, and I shall continue to dig pitfalls and string clotheslines along the lane to keep the somebodies under control. I'm told I got three necks and a collarbone last week, accounting for my cheerful countenance. Meantime, in a sort of controlled reprisal I'm making a double-runner. I hope to revive an interest in plain coasting and diminish the number of snowmobiles we must endure and the number of necks to break. I expect to be ready by the time snow flies. I plan to paint it red.

I despair when I look at the Christmas toy section in the new mail-order catalog. Somebody was telling me a few days ago about a man who had an office calculating machine and when it broke down he found it would be expensive to repair. So he bought a new one and gave the broken one to the local kindergarten for the tots to play with. The tots, being hep in this bright new world, repaired it and sold it for five hundred dollars. I believe this. The new-toy section in the catalog reads like a progress report from the Massachusetts Institute of Technology, and this year's boy in the six-to-eight age group is approaching the holiday in terms of urban renewal, environmental control, highrise engineering, space pioneering, and interplanetary communications. (Batteries not included; please order separately.) One toy, unique with a bucolic flavor, is a complete farm, advertised to inculcate useful lessons, and besides all the machinery it has a garden all planted. Just water it, and stand back to be educated. This is for the odd one, because there's got to be something out of joint with a modern boy who wants a field of oats for Christmas—and also with the society that has taken his playthings away. I'm wondering if perhaps the odd one will be vulnerable if I show up with a keen new bobsled and give him a push downhill.

Right now, my double-runner is nowhere near ready for sliding. I've had trouble finding a plank for a seat, to connect the two sleds. Time was you could get reliable maple or spruce at any lumberyard. Today you ask for a supple plank and the man says, "What would you want it for?" I say, "A bobsled," and then he asks what a bobsled is. Another thing—there isn't a blacksmith around to iron the runners. Time was, again, when every town had an ironworker. I've found some steel rods, and I'll try to fit them as runners. I'll see. I do have the red paint. And as I've worked on this project, I've enjoyed memories of all the gruesome things that happened when everybody turned out on a moonlit night to slide on Miller's Hill. Crisp and clear. How the night tingled with the elongated shouts of fun and the peals of laughter as whole families together shot down the long hill! On the way back uphill with every hand on the long rope it was well to keep off the "track," because down would come another family and swoosh by us. They, coming back, would stand aside while we, again, came down. Two or three slides, at the most, completed an evening's outing. Miller's Hill was about two miles.

But so has the bobsled faded that folks coming in to see what I'm making ask, "What-er-ya-makin'?" "Traverse runners," I say, which is what one of our Maine bobsleds was called. "A double-runner." Not all, but one now and then has said, "Oh, good! What fun those were." They were fun, but I find those who remember like to recall the disasters of winding the thing around a tree or shooting off into a brook. One fellow told how he ran his bobsled under a horse, which put the horse up on Lon Putney's front piazza. I was laboring in joy, but all comments were lugubrious. "Didn't you ever have a slide that came off pleasantly?" I'd ask.

"Oh, sure! But there was the night we had the schoolteacher on headlight and when we hit the stump she went into the snowbank out of sight! Nose first, she went, and closed the door!"

So the disasters were fun too. I do recall one night that we tangled with a stone wall and suddenly all my joyous, fun-loving friends were gone. Alone and bereft, I lugged the shattered front sled under one arm and tugged the other shambles by the string and got the wreck uphill and home. The next day my uncle repaired the sleds, good as new, and when I got to the hill my friends all returned. I have no memories of injuries except to the sled.

When I do get my bobsled ready, the big problem will be where to slide. Our old country roads, packed down for team sledding, are no longer available. Sand and salt and rubber wheels are incompatible with coasting. Lacking such, I do have a short incline that I can pack with a shovel well enough to show some young friend what it was like back when people had fun coasting. The slide should be long enough for youngsters up to, say, six. After that, they become consulting engineers, political economists, and high-rise architects. So the memories may be the best reward for my good intentions. I'll think about the one on front who was the headlight and the one to go first into the snowbank. Then the steerer, who had cleats for his feet and wound the pull-rope about his mittens. Then as many as could fit on the plank behind him, and on back the tailgate, who gave a push and then hopped on.

This youngster came into my shop and asked what I was making, and I told him how we would slide on it when I got it finished. He thought that would be exciting, and I was pleased. Then he said, "And we can use my father's snowmobile to pull it back uphill!"

42 Whatever Became of Dr. Tufts?

Maine's Town of Brunswick sits by the polluted Andro-scoggin River, and just lately a sign appeared by the Maine Street bridge protesting the stench of the watershed. This is by no means the first protest, but this sign is in context with the way things are done nowadays. Instead of grabbing a good issue by the throat and getting things done, we put up signs and hold meetings and make demonstrations, and get on TV as "resident," "witness," "relative," and other designations proving we are active and aware. It seems to me by this time we ought to be able to clean up a river—we've been working at it so long. The sign I saw hasn't helped yet.

Going-on fifty years ago, our Androscoggin River was as putrid as any on the North American continent. When the Magalloway River comes down from Parmachenee Lake and joins the outlet of Umbagog Lake, the confluence is the start of the Androscoggin, and the waters are sweet and serene. Then civilization butts in. Take 'em as they come—the paper mills at Berlin, New Hampshire, and at Rumford and Livermore / Jay, Maine, have poured their effluents into the stream to mingle with the raw sewage of every liberal community along the way down to generous Lewiston. There was, fifty years ago, no great public outcry over this disgrace—no big plea for clean waters. The combination of industrial chemistry and public disposal turned the flowing waters into a dead river, where no fish could live. People along the valley slept with wet rags over their faces, to fend off the stench. And Maine, as a guardian commonwealth obligated to look after its people and to perpetuate its assets, found nothing wrong with this and went on advertising for tourists.

Along about 1950, two things happened which should give us pause in this new era of signs and agitated petitions. The first efforts to do something about the stinking river appeared. First, there was Dr. Tufts. He was a horse doctor—a vet—and his practice took him up and down the Androscoggin River Valley. He, not so much as a professional man but as a concerned citizen, began promoting a new attitude and urging cleaner waters. He worked up a slide-lecture he gave to Granges and service clubs, and after a certain time he became known for his efforts. His slides were made along the river, showing debris and the effects of pollution, and none of them was complimentary to those individuals and industries which were causing the problem. Dr. Tufts very soon became the traditional thorn in the side of those who would have to snap out of it and clean up the Androscoggin if Dr. Tufts were to succeed in his crusade. So you may well ask whatever became of Dr. Tufts. I do not know. He went somewhere else, and as he was then a young man it is likely he is still there. First, the gentle suggestion came to him by devious indirections that he would do well to keep his mouth shut—that certain vested interests were not pleased by his remarks and he was a trouble maker. When Dr. Tufts continued to show his slides, rather than to listen to good advice, a strange thing happened. All at once his good friends who kept animals and had called him to attend cats, dogs, cows, horses, and even myna birds started calling in veterinary talent from far places, and even passed him by on the street without a nod. The word had gone forth, and a fat paycheck counteracts a fat stink. Industry had girded its loins. Dr. Tufts left Maine.

The second thing that happened about then was the complaint of Joe Annicetti. Joe had come from Italy before the World War and settled in Lisbon Falls, on the bank of the rushing Androscoggin, to operate a fruit stand. Joe's grandson still operates it at the same place. Joe prospered, and one day decided to put a new coat of paint on his building. This was done—an off-white cream color that suited the building and the location, and everybody told Joe it was a great improvement and a credit to the town. But after a few weeks this pleasant cream color shifted to a somewhat reddish brown, and Joe didn't like reddish brown. Neither did the townspeople, and Joe's reddish brown was quickly dubbed a "calf-turd brindle." Joe complained at the Bailey Hardware Store, where he'd bought the paint, and Mr. Bailey complained to the jobber, and the jobber to the manufacturer, and shortly a trouble-shooter came to see what was going on. Joe, who never mastered English too well, gesticulated with more italiano than finesse, but conveyed the idea that he was not happy. The trouble-shooter looked at the building, scraped off some bits of paint, and said he would be back.

Analysis in a laboratory showed that chemicals thrown off by the polluted Androscoggin River had caused the change in color.

But instead of going after the cause of pollution, the paint people chose to produce a new formula designed specifically for use in the Androscoggin Valley. We now had two kinds of paint—one for everybody else, and one for the Androscoggin people. Joe got his building redone with the new kind and he was happy, although he still slept at night with a wet rag.

All the efforts at improving the quality of the Androscoggin have been pretty much of that stripe. Just a few miles above Lewiston the Central Maine Power Company has a hydroelectric station—Gulf Island Dam. Generating electricity is not a cause of pollution in itself, but the water-storage basin acted as a host for the pollution that was coming down the river. Anything in the water would settle, and then after it reacted to its own enzymes it would surge and resurge and come boiling to the surface. Having released its goodies in all directions, thus exhausting its wallop, it would settle and await another regurgitation. The power company had nothing to do with this, in a way, but it joined in an expensive effort to find a solution. The solution was to pour more chemicals into the water, to rectify those already working, and for years a boat was maintained, a supply of chemicals kept ready, and a crew regularly applied the remedy. Industry did some bragging about this valiant effort, which was likened to shaking talcum powder into a four-hole backhouse.

Then came our first clean-waters bill. The legislator who introduced it explained that it was something he did "by request" and he really hadn't yet made up his own mind. Leery. Remember Dr. Tufts? The wording of the bill was all right. It said, in effect, that "all the waters of the State of Maine shall be clean." A good beginning! In due time the bill was sent to committee, and the members of the committee began hearing all the things that were said to them by the people who ran the mills. They heard how much this would cost. Mills would have to go into bankruptcy. Think of the jobs to be lost! These things were not necessarily said, you understand, officially. People who went to the public hearing showed a disposition to like clean waters, but over at the Augusta House, in the evening . . . The first Maine clean-waters bill was finally reported "Ought to Pass" by the committee! Ah, sweet Victory!

There had been a mite of monkey-business with the bill. It had been amended. Now it said, "all the waters of the state shall be clean EXCEPT THOSE ALREADY PART OF AN EXISTING WATERSHED."

Mainers, truth to tell, are accustomed to such legislative shenanigans, so that was all right. The law was passed. Any of the elected legislators connected with this, and all the mill owners, were eager to protest that they love their State of Maine.

But anything of that sort will have its day and then comes a reckoning. By this time enough people wanted to clean up the Androscoggin so we got a lawsuit. The idea was to get a judge to order the dirty ones to tidy up. This was aimed at industry, of course, but there was sense in this. The mill effluvia was causing the river to resist the normal propensity of running water to purify itself. The river might not fend off all the offal from human discharge, but given a chance it would take care of some of it. The mill waste was primary, sewage secondary. So the argument ran. Industry by now had the state's best legal talent sewed up, and this galaxy was able to get the trial set "in vacation." This got all the sitting judges off the hook, which pleased them, and left things to an old gaffer who was simply ideal. He was retired, and soft as a custard, but in the Maine judicial system he was available under a thing called "active retired." He had long since forgotten how to tie his shoes, and had to ask directions when he went to the toilet. He really did wear carpet slippers when he presided. He handled this trial, and it was clearly a matter of the job seeking the man.

Since "in vacation" meant the summertime, and the courthouse stood not far from the Androscoggin River in Auburn, the massive testimony to prove that the Androscoggin River did not stink was permeated throughout by the stench coming in the courtroom windows. The plaintiffs noticed this. But numerous willing witnesses, who gladly testified even though they worked in the mills, affirmed that the Androscoggin River was indeed a bed of roses and they didn't smell anything. Lady Law had things well in hand. But at this moment the senile old judge, half asleep and not paying attention to the evidence, roused and beckoned to a bailiff. The bailiff then went and got a long pole with a hook on it and he closed all the courtroom windows. So it was pleasantly diverting, later, when the judge found for industry, as everybody knew he would, and the sponsors of clean waters went home after their day in court. There was a good feeling throughout Maine at the assurance our well being was in the hands of a justice that couldn't tie shoe laces.

There may be those who will carp at my contentions, but let them first notice that fifty years have passed and that sign was there. The difference is that today there isn't anything funny about dirty water. In the good old days, at least we could chuckle when we saw the bailiff closing the windows.

43 Where Would You Find a Dust Cap?

Doc Rockwell, the forgotten vaudeville actor, went to a boatbuilder over at East Boothbay and said, "My gorries, Egstrom, how does your wife find time to do all she does? She's in the PTA, and belongs to the Ladies' Aid. She's librarian, treasurer of the church, substitutes as schoolteacher, runs the playground program, is secretary of the extension, coaches the choir, heads up the Washington trip, drives the senior citizen bus, handles lunches for shut-ins, does the Cancer drive, does the Easter seals, and God knows what else. How does she find time?"

Egstrom said, "She don't dust."

I am about to mention a dust cap, and I've paused to wonder if anybody knows what a dust cap is.

Since our Middle-east friends contrived to hoist the prices of petroleum products, Maine has turned back to wood-burning parlor stoves. When you stop and think of it, Maine folks made a mistake when they embraced fuel oil. We are the most forested of the states, wood is a renewable asset, and every year more wood goes to waste in our wilderness than we'd use to keep all outdoors at 78° F. Perhaps we got lazy and became allergic to the chainsaw. All at once we had the blessing of oil heat, and then all at once we began setting up stoves again. Dust caps go with wood stoves.

That opens a meditative corridor. The subject, no doubt, is "Stove Day." And, along with dust caps, what became of sweet oil? I've asked, and conclude that sweet oil has disappeared from the market. We lost a lot of lore that went with sweet oil. My dictionary says that sweet oil is olive oil, but it isn't. I don't know what it was, but it came in a little bottle and we went and bought a bottle for Stove Day. Spring Stove Day. We had a Stove Day in the spring when the stove was taken out of the parlor and stored in the shed for summer, and another in the fall when it was brought back into the parlor and set up for the winter. The stove was well anointed with sweet oil so it wouldn't rust during the summer.

So we'll not really get the good out of our modern, oil-saving space heaters until we've found a bottle of sweet oil and made the traditional ceremony. The kitchen range served the utility side of housekeeping and remained in place—it didn't get "taken out" and "put back." Heat in bedrooms? Certainly—if it seeped in from the parlor or kitchen. Bathrooms? What bathrooms? And come to think of it, you need a wing. A wing, a dust cap, and some sweet oil.

The wing of a hen or rooster that was lately invited to dinner. As a brush. Nobody had vacuum cleaners in the days of stoves, so ashes were cleaned out with a wing. The chauviniste who femaled the housecleaning couldn't get along without wings. And there would come the morning that she would pull her dust cap down over her ears, assume a purposeful and belligerent manner, proclaim that Stove Day was at hand, and defy anybody to interfere. Summerizing the stove was something to be put off as long as possible, because in Maine spring lingers in the lap of winter, and the best you can do is guess close. It was not a day Mother tackled with glee, and the menfolks dreaded it.

First, the ashes were removed, completely. With a shovel, then with a brush, and then with the wing. To the last bit. The stove had been "let out" so there were no hot embers. Grape vines like wood ashes, so we took them in a pail and scattered them under the arbor. Rousting up the ashes that way made like a fogmull in the parlor, and although Mother knew there was only one way to take out ashes, she warned against making a mess. Next, the flue pipe was disconnected from the back of the stove and from the thimble in the chimney, and before it leaked too much soot on the floor it would have the stove end shoved into a pail. It took two people to pick up the pail and the flue and waltz them into the dooryard. Banging the tin pipe with a stick made the soot come loose, and the menfolks giving their all to this could hear Mother from the parlor as she bemoaned how clumsy men can be. Now the stove could be moved, and out it went into the warm spring sunlight to get its sweet oil. The parlor would be cleansed thoroughly, and the marble-top stand moved over to the spot where the stove passed the winter.

The sweet oil did have a "sickie-sweet" smell, and it could be felt all over the dooryard. Sunlight dried the oil somewhat, and then the stove was put in a corner of the shed and covered with a horse blanket. Horses don't need blankets in the summer. Thus in repose the stove estivated. Meantime, back in the parlor, the stuffiness of winter was gone. Fresh and clean, aired out, and the windows open, the parlor was a brand new place, as much a sign of spring as crocuses and fiddlehead ferns. That's half the story of the old wood-burning days. The spring Stove Day was over, and Mother could take off her dust cap. All evening she would complain about the taste of ashes and soot in her mouth, and understandingly would remind that Job, with all his troubles, had the same complaint.

Sweet oil was not stove blacking. It would lose some of its greasiness as summer wore along, but not much of its odor. Under the horse blanket it bided, and anybody passing near could assume that the parlor stove was ready for fall. Whichever day Mother picked for fall Stove Day was never dusty and sooty, and making ready called only for moving the marble-top stand. In came the stove, it was set on the tin fireguard and the flue connected to the chimney. Some birch bark and dry cedar kindlings were laid in, the woodbox filled with maple and beech, and the family was ready for the first fall evening when it got cool around the edges and a fire would feel good. This would be the happy wood-burning evening that today's converts from fuel oil should know about.

It can't really be described and explained. You had to be there. The birch bark would get lit, and the cedar kindlings would catch, and a couple of sticks from the woodbox would be inserted. The stove would get hot. And the heat would "burn off" the residual sweet oil. There is, as far as I know, no stench to challenge this one. It was horrid. And it would linger well onto Christmas, and rise up to strike again. Opening windows didn't help a bit. True, there wasn't a lick of rust on the stove after its summer in the shed, which was the thing to say about sweet oil. And once the sweet oil had burned off, Mother—the next morning—would "black" the stove. She used a paste from a can and an old rag. I'm told this paste is lacking today, as is sweet oil—and wings and dust caps. Now the family settled in for happy evenings that would continue until spring Stove Day.

Oh, yes—how about these advertisements that tell us you can hardly tell the stuff from butter? It's not necessarily so. My friend

Flint Johnson used to have a woods camp up on Eustis Ridge, and in the fall he'd guide for deer hunting. So one year Flint asked me if I'd like to ride up to Eustis Ridge with him while he made the camp ready for hunting. This was August, so we planned on a trout chowder out of Parker Stream, and off we went. We got the trout, and washed all the dishes, and made the beds, and swept up, and filled the lamps and the woodbox, and shortly everything was ready for the sports to come and go hunting. We had the trout ready, and Flint loaded up the Kineo range and started a fire.

Well, sir—you talk about burning off a stove! That stove caught, and a blue pall of clear quill filled the camp so we had to step outside to breathe. Stink? I guess it stunk. It was the grand-daddy of all Capitalized Stench. When I caught my breath I said, "That ain't sweet oil!"

"No," says Flint. "I forgot to bring any sweet oil, so I had to use something else when I greased the stove last spring."

"What?"

"Well, all I had was a square of margarine left over from hunting season."

"Margarine?"

"Eyah," says Flint. "Can't hardly tell it from butt-teh, can you?"

44 Something to Do in February

An editor who is kind to me writes to suggest I "think summer." Today is February 3rd. Editors like to keep well ahead, and this one is already deciding on his July issues, and he means that he would like to have something from me appropriate to July. Along in August he will begin to "think Christmas." So I'm trying to think summer in February, and there came to mind that June wedding last year when the bridal party snowshoed to church. I think it was back in 1938 that I began thinking summer most of the time. I had been down cellar fixing the water pump and missed summer altogether. It was on a Tuesday. Several people who told me about it said it was a remarkable summer, first to last. So I've been hoping ever since to see a Maine summer. Maybe this is the year, if I think hard enough. Some say the seasons are changing.

Maybe. It's true our January thaw came in May last year, instead of April. This threw off our timing and it took months to adjust. Into the middle of June we had such a light snow cover that most people put up their skiddoos for a time, planning only to have them ready in August for blueberrying. A good way to explain a Maine summer is to say that when warmer days come our highway crews take the snow blades off the trucks, but leave the hydraulic mechanism in place for quick re-attachment if we have a blizzard during the Fourth of July tourist peak. Since this custom was put in practice we've had hardly any summer visitors stranded at our resorts.

This is entirely a manner of speaking. We have as much summer as anybody, meaning the period from the solstice to the equinox. We often have a hot spell all day, so geraniums may be put out on the porch if brought in by late afternoon. When we had that heavy frost last August our newspapers printed a good many letters to the editor. Some said it was the last frost of spring, and others thought it was the first frost of fall. The speculation was only amusing; it made little difference. Whatever else may be deplored, we do not have the tiresome procession of weather after weather that goes with living elsewhere. It is refreshing indeed to hoe tomatoes in the garden in the heat of the day, and then take the family to the lighted ski slope in the evening for a family romp in the brisk air.

Some seasons ago, when the Fort Fairfield *Review* was still

Maine's most reliable publication, that paper had an account of a wedding that was originally scheduled for "the first comfortable June day." That turned out to be the 15th. The spacious lawn of the bride's residence on Currier Street had been cleared of snow, and the double-ring ceremony was held under an evergreen arch beside a bonfire. The reporter described the L. L. Bean parkas worn by the bride and her attendants, and the larrigans and mackinaw of the bridegroom. The Rev. Mr. Arthur Tuttle had on black and red double-knit mittens in the fox-and-geese pattern. Deviating from custom, the bride's mother wore skis rather than the traditional bear paw snowshoes.

Thus it is, and I'm taking a risk by "thinking summer" in this way—I'm sure many people will imagine I'm making this all up out of heavy woolen cloth. But I'm not—this is routine summer thinking for a Maine February. When there's no ice in the bird bath we're having a heat wave. We, who wouldn't dip in the ocean to win a million-dollar bet, enjoy watching the summer people standing on the beach in their swim suits and fur coats. Why do you suppose the resort hotels by the ocean have those signs—"Surf Bathing & Hot Showers"? Harold Jameson, my lobstering neighbor, went through the ice in January and "closed the door," as they say. Harold got out all right and warmed up in a week or so. He said, "You got to realize, it ain't no colder down there now than it'll be come sum-muh!"

We Mainers think summer more than we should, and talk about it a lot. We realize that if the seasons do change and we get a warming trend, life in the Pine Tree State will lose some of its long-time joy. It isn't every state where people think summer and chip the ice away from the hotbed. We water our tender garden seedlings in the coldframe and put a blanket over the glass at night. And then we think summer some more. All summer long we think summer, and when it gets bleak and drab in July and the pipes catch in the barn, we think again about summer—either last summer or next. Past or present, it matters little—summer in Maine is something to think about.

45 Keep out of the Hot Sun

A plaintive letter came not long ago from David Hanson, who wrote that he hopes to find a home in Maine, or a place to build one, and he wonders why we Mainers have been reluctant to turn to the sun for domestic heat. This is a good question. Here and there an effort has been made, and not always on new houses, but I suspect for the most part we linger sentimentally with the old contention that it takes a few sticks of dry alder to brown cream-tartar biscuits. This may not be logic, but it works on biscuits. I'll hazard that the greatest astronomers know less about browning biscuits than I do. I wrote to Mr. Hanson and told him I knew only two things.

One is that long years ago, before anybody began talking about solar heat, it was in use at Ogunquit. David Woodbury, the writer, inherited the Ogunquit home of his father, the artist, and the only heat the place had came from the sun. David was an M.I.T. engineer, but his paint-brush father had planned the house while David was a tot. Winter and summer the house was comfortable. The equipment had a hold-over tank, so even after several days of an Ogunquit fogmull water would be scalding hot. I visited David and his wife, India, there, and David showed me how the thing worked. First time I was aware of solar heat of that sort.

The other thing is that Maine has more hours of sunlight in

the winter than any of our more advertised sun spots. Florida, for one place, isn't even close. The United States weather bureau stated this for a fact back in the early years of the 1900s, and our tourist bureau picked it up and made a lot of it. It may, of course, be forty below zero in Fort Kent, but the sun is out. It takes a mite of equivocation to relate Maine sunshine to warmth. You can't blame an honest Mainer if he comes in with his mittens frozen to his hands, the sun bright but weak in a slate-blue sky, and doubts if a sun machine would make his kitchen cozy. But, it will—or would—and there are, indeed, other ways to brown a pan of biscuits. The day may come.

When Mr. Hanson's good letter came, I thought at once of Joe Giguerre. World War II was kind to Joe. He finished building a house just before Pearl Harbor, and applied to our Central Maine Power Company for service. Just then the war broke, and certain restrictions went into effect. Joe had applied "under the wire," so a crew came and ran a line to his house. But the War Production Board, or the OPA or something, had put electric meters on the no-no list, and there was Joe all hooked up to the generating plant and the power company had no meter to put on his line. During the war, and for three years afterwards, Joe faithfully paid his monthly electric bill gladly. He was, all that time, on the one dollar a month minimum charge. It was pleasant to go into Joe's house on a deepdown January morning and find all the burners, and the oven, of his electric range at full blast. When Mrs. Joe wanted to brown a pan of biscuits, she had to shut the oven door first and let things cool down. When the war was over and meters were again available, Joe installed oil heat in his basement.

Joe told me, "When Rosie bakes, she shut the oven door and the house goes cold."

In my wonderful youth, the answer to thermal comfort was to stand on a chair. The oven door on the Modern Clarion wood-burning kitchen range was my salvation. Mother would be making breakfast, but she condescended and the chair stood in front of the open oven door and she fried eggs and stirred the oatmeal around it. One by one, we youngsters got up on the chair to dress. The heat from the oven came out at just that height above the floor. The floor was cold and the ceiling hadn't warmed. Chair-level was great. The acrobatic agility required to stand on a chair and get both legs into a pair of pants has been exceeded only by acts in the circus. "Hurry up," Mother would say, "your egg's ready." I was going-on fourteen when Mother suggested one day that I might be a little old to dress on a chair. My father laughed and said he dressed on a chair until he was twenty-eight.

The evening was the best time for the kitchen stove oven. With a hearth on front and a ledge across the side under the oven door, there was room for a family's feet. An uncle had his rocker so he could put his feet up on the hearth, and Old Timer, the stub-tailed, battle-scarred tomcat, would stretch out on his thigh. Uncle liked to read western stories. Every now and then the cat would twinge his claws through Uncle's pants and grab a knee, whereat Uncle would swat the cat with the magazine. Old Timer was punchie. The rest of us would perch as we could, oven door open, and we'd do school work or fancy work or read. Apples and popcorn. There was a wire over the stove on which we dried mittens and socks, and very wet items would be laid over the top of the open oven door. All cozy and good, and warm—even steamy. Every now and then somebody would stand up and turn his mittens over. In the oven, evenings, would be my stick of beech wood in a flannel bag—getting ready to warm my feet when I went to bed. Maybe my best memory is of those evenings around the open oven, serene with happiness and family love, taking a bite from a crispy Northern Spy apple, and then opening the *Gallic Wars* to see what Caesar did today. Maybe I won't convince Mr. Hanson, but my oven of boyhood wasn't 92,000,000 miles away.

46 Beedy Served Four Terms

Maine has never been the same since the congressmen stopped sending free garden seeds. Other states can probably say the same. The subject was brought up by Roddy Tomkins when we met in the post office. Roddy said, "I was reading that pussyflage you wrote about plarntin' gardens and I thought you was going to say something about the free seeds we used to get from congressmen. How come you din't say nawthin' 'bout gettin' free seeds from congressmen?"

Roddy has an A.B. degree, English major, from Yale, but he talks that way on account of the summer people. He says if he talks real Maine, he can get ten dollars more a week on the beach cottages he rents.

I said, "Trade secret. If I tell you, you'll blab it all over town, and everybody in town will start being a writer."

"Everybody in town already *is* a writer," says Roddy.

"All right. The reason is I didn't think of it. But I still wouldn't of if I'd thought of it."

"Wouldn't have," said Roddy. "Why not?"

"Because it don't pay to shoot off all your fireworks in one big bang. Free seeds from congressmen will give me another whole piece. I could write one good yarn that would cover every subject under the sun, but what about tomorrow? The way I work it, I always have something for next time. I thank you for bringing the subject up; I'll attend to it soon."

"Bringing up the subject," said Roddy. "You know better than that."

"Eyah."

Then I said, "How long would you say it's been since congressmen sent free seeds?"

"I'm guessing around 1930. P'aps the depression had something to do with it. After that Roosevelt got in and we had a plague of Democrats, and I'm pretty sure I got my last free seeds from a Republican. Name was Beedy. He was a lawyer, and worse than that—he came from Portland. Prolly wouldn't of known a marigold from a swamp maple, but he always sent me free seeds."

"Wouldn't *have* known," I said.

"Ayeh."

"Were they any good?"

"Very good. They came in little packages marked 'Not for Sale' and instead of coming to boxholder they really had my name on 'em. Those were good times back when your congressman knew your name. Nowadays I'm just boxholder or current resident. Even occupant. The Federal Government hasn't been folksy since it went out of the seed business. There was something about seeds. I recall the year Beedy sent me some okra seeds. Got me all fired up. I didn't know anything about okra, but now I had a great hanker to grow some. But I didn't. Seeds didn't sprout. Everything else sprouted, but no okra. I was some disappointed not to find out what okra is."

"It's a mallow, grown for its mucilaginous pods—used in soups. Never does well here in Maine."

"Is that so? Well, for a Portland lawyer Beedy did all right. Those seeds were supplied to congressman by the Department of Agriculture—didn't cost the congressman a cent, and postage was free—so I suppose I had no reason to suspect Beedy would know anything about okra. He tried and I tried. I watched all summer for my okra to come up. Not a sprout. But the next election I walked two miles in a rainstorm to vote for Beedy."

"I think Beedy served four terms altogether."

"Give the credit to seeds. The first year he quit on seeds he lost the election. I guess nowadays nobody can really appreciate what those seeds meant. People were feet-up at the kitchen stove, dawdlin' out the doldrums of Febbu-wary, and the mailman would come jinglin' up with the *Country Gentleman*, the interest notice from the bank, and a batch of seeds from the congressman. Nothing like seeds in February! Put new life into everybody. I'd shove another stick in the stove and fondle them seeds and dream about hoeing through a hot June. The country was in good hands. Congress was in touch with the farmer. Nawthin's been the same since."

"Don't you suppose the people in the seed business lobbied to protect their interests?"

"Prolly. But a congressman has interests, too. You got to wonder about the intelligence of a congressman that will vote himself out of a sure thing. Shouldn't of done it."

"Shouldn't *have*."

"You write it your way and I'll speak it mine. Mucilaginous. So that's okra! Just as well it never sprouted."

"'Eyah."

47 Always Take Store Money

As the old order changed, we've had a proliferation of "country" stores; some of 'em send catalogs and invite purchases by mail. This is good, but with all due respect if you want a pitcher pump or a No. 2 lamp chimney, you may find these proprietors are stretching the definitions. The true country stores these entrepreneurs are imitating are as dead as the last lingering dodo, and in a very real way we are asked to trade with imposters. Let's wish 'em prosperity. A country store did much more than offer penny candy and pickles out of a barrel, wheel cheese and tub butter and salt-slacked pollock. What's more, if one of these modern country stores does have those oddities, veracity and verisimilitude are wanting. Oh, well . . . If you want to compare one of these new-day emporia to the real thing of long ago—ask one of them if it'll take a bushel of cucumbers for store money. That's a good test.

Store money was for taking out in trade. Stores used to buy things from farmers, but today there has to be a broker and somebody from the bank and delivery is by truckload at Lancaster, Pennsylvania. The day is gone when the manager of the local Magic-Saver Super can buy in a few heads of lettuce. You'll travel far before you'll find a grocer today who knows what store money was. Food stamps and check cashing machines and scanners. And show me a modern, enterprising storekeeper who lets even his best customer take a bag of groceries home on tick! Store money!

I was peddling small sass from my 4-H Club garden when I first encountered store money. Mr. Magoun, who didn't live to know what a charge card would be, looked over his counter and over his half-moon spectacles to eye my little basket of rosy-red vine-ripe John Baer tomatoes. He saw that they were good. "I'll take 'em! Two cents a pound, two-and-a-half store money."

I didn't know about store money, so I took the cash and went home to ask my father. "Always take store money," he said. It means you'll get your money as you buy things at the store. My father said he always took store money. He got a half a cent or so extra when he did, and Mr. Magoun was happy because he had his wholesale-retail margin to play around with. My father applied his store money when he paid his weekly store bill—and, all right, got his "treat." After that, I took store money, and it would be applied to Dad's account, and then Dad would give me real money. I "made" that way, and everybody was pleased. The one fault with store money is that you never get to jingle it in your pocket. The treat was standard at country stores. Upon paying his bill the customer got a cigar if he smoked, or a small sack of two–three vanilla creams to take home to the missus. If I were with Dad when he paid, Mr. Magoun might let me take a pickle from the barrel. Bauer Small, who kept the W. W. Small general store in Farmington, had a "jug" in a refrigerator out back, and customers who paid could have a "honk." The honking customers knew where the jug was and would step out back and help themselves.

Mr. Magoun, and other storekeepers, sometimes got caught up on store money and had to be careful. Well, if a good customer came in and said, "Mr. Magoun, would you like to take a few nice fresh hens' eggs?" Mr. Magoun might not need any nice fresh hens' eggs at the moment, but he couldn't take risks with a good customer. Eggs that sit around too long lose their appeal. My Uncle Ralph, who kept a country store, used to tell about the farmer who worked off a case of rotten eggs on him, and when spoken to sharply about it said, "Well, damn a hen that'll lay rotten eggs!"

One time a little lady came into Uncle Ralph's store to ask if he'd take a bushel of beechnuts. Beechnuts come in a small triangular shell, and pop out of the burr at the first sharp frost in September. They're the dickens to find under the tree, and Uncle Ralph was dubious that anybody would have a bushel of the things all at once. But the lady had a bushel measure full of beechnuts, and Uncle Ralph said he'd take them. Then came the question of what a bushel of beechnuts should fetch. "What will you pay me?" the little lady asked.

Uncle Ralph said, "I'll be as generous as I can—how much were you expecting to get?"

"Well, I was hoping to get at least fifty cents."

Uncle Ralph gave her a dollar, and he'd put eight or ten of the delicious little nuts in a candy bag and hand them out as treats. Made a big hit, and everybody was amazed that the little lady had managed to gather a full bushel. Uncle Ralph never saw her before, and never saw her again.

Another of Uncle Ralph's stories about store money had to do with the farmer who brought in a bushel of yellow-eye beans. They make a favorite Maine baked bean. "Glad to get 'em," said Uncle Ralph, "I'll put 'em to your account."

He did—he went right to the register and put in a slip, "Credit, by one bu. YE beans, $2.50." But a couple of days later he started to put the beans in two-pound bags, and he found they hadn't been well "picked-over." The farmer had swept up the barn floor after threshing, and barn floors, best you can do, yield hen manure. Uncle Ralph went back to the register and corrected the slip. Now he wrote, "Credit, by one bu. hen manure. 10¢."

The farmer made an effort at remonstrance when they settled up, but Uncle Ralph said, "Federal law requires that all food show the principal ingredients."

The country store is indeed long gone. It's good to have these make-believe country stores, and I'm glad they'll honor a Visa card.

48 Uncle Ralph Had Four Prices

Store money was good money. In those days, any money was good. Today we talk about inflation but what we mean is that our money is no good. Two things lately came to my attention. First, the outdoor magazine told me that the estate auctioned Gus Garcelon's collection of firearms, and that his Winchester 45:70 rifle fetched $65,000. I'm glad, because I have a Winchester 40:65, which is a comparable piece in an antique series, and if mine is worth half of that I'm ready to do business. Ammunition for guns of that series hasn't been available for years, unless you want to load your own, so in a way a 40:65 is worthless except to a museum or to a collector with independent income. I used to hunt with the gun when I could buy cartridges. It was heavy to lug through the woods, but it had a wallop that provided food if a deer offered his services. The gun is long retired. Then, about the same time as that gun auction, the telephone company wrote me that it was instituting a new service that would help businessmen collect accounts receivable.

This letter doesn't say what this has to do with running a telephone company, and probably has nothing to do with it, but it is news to me that any businessman has accounts receivable. Accounts receivable went out of style when the banks invented the charge card. I had all this explained to me by my garageman. I bought my pick-up truck from him, and every so often I would take it back to him for what Joe Gamache calls "a periodic check-up from time to time." Also, to get a state inspection sticker. This is a functional review, and it became a social occasion because I would sit and talk with my garageman while his executioner opened the hood and generated about fifty dollars' worth of fiddling around. When I left, I would have the oil changed, the windshield inflated, and a bill. I would take the bill home and pass it to my household treasurer. She would make out a check and I would mail it the next morning. In this way my garageman and I had a pleasant association of many agreeable years. He did his part and I paid promptly. Then one day I got an improbable letter from my garageman, and a new day had dawned.

He told me, and the form letter told all his customers, that henceforth cash over the counter was the only alternative to my having a credit card. He even told me which credit card it had to be—indicating clearly that he was being pushed by somebody. Later he revised this limitation, and I assumed Master

Charge and Visa and American Express had reached him. He was heartbroken to have to do this, he said, but without such-and-such a credit card I couldn't do business with him. Stupid as this sounds, it is exactly what he said. So there I was, a perfectly good customer of long standing, an upright citizen with no debts and money in the Credit Union. My former garageman explained to me that this was forced upon him by his bank, which saw a big future in credit cards and had everything figured out. They told him they would no longer accept his "accounts receivable" as collateral on business loans, thus making it impossible for him to finance his own garage as he had been doing. They would collect his accounts receivable, take their cut, and get the lovely 18 percent on overdue balances. All he had to do was tell me to go get a charge card. Friendship and goodwill had nothing to do with anything. My former garageman told me, "Don't feel so bad—I didn't have any choice either."

But I did have a choice. The next time my pick-up was due, I found me a barnyard mechanic back in the country and he has served me since. I'm told he keeps his money in nail kegs in the barn attic. So I began to wonder what the telephone company is trying to prove. What accounts receivable? I've mentioned my Uncle Ralph, the storekeeper. Uncle Ralph used his accounts receivable all the years he was in business—to his own prosperity and that of his bank. Uncle Ralph used to say that Wall Street offered no investment opportunity as good as 2 percent for cash in ten days. If you can take in 2 percent on your capital every ten days you've got it made. About extending credit, some of Uncle Ralph's customers complained that he had "two prices." He denied this. He said, "I have four prices." First was the price to a cash customer with money in his hand. Next, to the good customer who bought on credit but paid faithfully every payday. Then to the customer who was slow, paying something now and again but never cleaning up all that he owed. And fourth was the man who would avoid payment and perhaps would be sued. It is the fourth of these to whom I owe a thank-you. Because he didn't pay Uncle Ralph, I got the Winchester 40:65 rifle.

All these folks have long since passed to their just reward, so I can use their names. Joe Punty was my Uncle Ralph's deadbeat customer. He worked in the woods and wasn't home often. His wife would come into the store and tell how her babies were hungry, and Uncle Ralph would let her have some groceries. He'd make her promise that she'd send Joe in to settle up, but Uncle Ralph hadn't seen Joe in years. It came to be a community joke that Uncle Ralph cased the Punty home regularly hoping to find Joe in residence. Then, one day, Percy Grimes came into the store to say, "Ralph—I'm here to do business! You give me a plug of Five Brothers eatin' tobacco, and I'll tell you something you want to know."

Thus Uncle Ralph was informed that Joe Punty was home. Uncle Ralph thumped on Joe's front door and then ran around to be at the back door when Joe tried to make his escape. They came to an agreement. Uncle Ralph would take whatever Joe had that was worth anything, and apply the value to Joe's account. And that was the day I arrived to visit Uncle Ralph for a few days and we would explore the trout brooks. At the store a clerk told me he was up at Joe Punty's, and I intercepted Uncle Ralph on his way back to the store. He looked like a peripatetic flea market.

He made me think of Chester Cahoon, the fireman who saved so many things when the Jenkins's house burned up at Tutts-ville. Holman Day wrote the poem. 'Twas a desperate case, and the firemen didn't know what to do. But Chester Cahoon went into the house, and shortly appeared at a second-floor window, surrounded by flame.

> He had in his hands, Sis, a stove and a bed,
> And he balanced a bureau right square on his head.
> His arms, they was loaded with crockery stuff—
> China and glassware, an' as if that warn't enough
> He had rolls of big quilts round his head like a wreath,
> And he carried Miz Jenkins old aunt with his teeth.

Uncle Ralph was loaded for fair, and had cleaned poor Joe Punty right out. He had a kerosene barn lantern and a canoe paddle. He was wearing a buffalo fur coat. And with everything else, he was dangling this 40:65 Winchester rifle by the trigger guard.

"Good to see you—I'll shake hands when I can set this junk down," he said, and I turned to walk along with him. I took a few items to help, and one of them was the rifle.

The 40:65 was a favorite game weapon in Maine in the old days of "meatmen." Lumber camps would hire a hunter to keep the camp supplied with fresh meat, and such a hunter was the "meatman." So Joe had this 40:65 when he had been a meatman, and Uncle Ralph allowed him $2.50 for it.

I looked the gun over and it was in good condition. The bore was clean, and the action smooth. I handed Uncle Ralph three dollars and said I'd take the gun. He said, "Keep your money. It's a present from me. And I'm tickled silly to get even that out of that son-of-a-bitch."

I said, "The customer is always right."

So there is much to be said for extending credit, and keeping your bills paid, and probably there is a dandy argument for charge cards. I've been wondering what the telephone company would do about collecting an account receivable from Joe Punty. How would the Supreme National Bank figure its 18 percent a month on a 40:65 Winchester? You know and I know that there isn't a banker in Maine who would finance $65,000 on a $2.50 gun that doesn't have any bullets. Or even half of that.

On second thought, if somebody wants my 40:65 lever-action Winchester at $65,000—I will gladly allow 2 percent for cash in ten days.

49 Remember the Registered Maine Guide?

Civilizations decline, cultures evaporate, and empires disappear for complicated reasons any historian will gladly elucidate at the drop of a federal grant, but this is a lot of foolishness. Things go to hell for smallish and, at the time, imperceptible reasons that nobody notices. One little mistake leads to another and a trend develops until after many days there is no turning back. Then things go into a smash and we no longer have a Holy Roman Empire, or any high school children who can spell, or any rabbits in the swamp or any mallards in the cove, and nobody in the legislature who can pronounce no. A much more than good argument can be served up to prove that Maine started down the sluice when the Registered Maine Guide was taken seriously. That was a smallish thing, but it was a portion of a pile with a magnificent downhill cant. The rest of the story comes at a brisk trot. (See Habakkuk in the Old Testament, Book two, Verse two.)

In a way this started with the good intentions of Governor Ralph O. Brewster, in 1925. He was astute, and went on to a brilliant career in Washington, D.C., in the House and Senate. He succeeded the amiable and philanthropic Governor Percival P. Baxter—a hard man to follow. In his campaign speeches, Brewster had promised to do something about "tourism," about which nobody in Maine had ever given a thought. Governor Brewster wanted to exploit our lakes and streams, our mountains and seashore, our hunting and fishing, and even the deep-down, good-natured, friendly down-easters. He foretold untold millions in blessed riches we would enjoy as we shared our birthright. Henry Ford had put America on wheels, and prosperity would be ours just as soon as we set up the Maine Publicity Bureau. Governor Brewster didn't say anything about the highways and bridges we would have to build, and he didn't enumerate any of the numerous drawbacks that went with such prosperity. We let the first little thing, and the second little thing, and we didn't expect all those little things to add up to what we have now. The Registered Maine Guide is somewhat symbolic of the way things went.

In a sense, to be honest, there really never was a Registered Maine Guide. Long before people were attracted to Maine by Governor Brewster, hunting and fishing had brought us many good friends who were far from "tourists." They came after ice-out in the spring and again in September and October to angle for the trout and salmon, and in November to get a deer. True, we had our "seasonal folks" at Bar Harbor and other early resorts, but they had little to do with Maine Guides. The hunters and fishers who came from the Philadelphias needed somebody to row boats and clean fish, to cook and tidy, to be nursemaid and valet, to dress the deer and mix the drinks, and thus necessity created the Maine Guide. He wasn't "registered," and except when he had a "'sport" in tow he wasn't thought of as a guide. In off-season he cooked in a lumber camp, taught school, and maybe drove the stage down to Rumford. But as time ran along, the "Maine Guide" became a big hero to the sports. When they went back to Philadelphia they told the yarns the guide had recited in the still of the evening with cigars and whiskey by the Franklin stove, and the Maine Guide became a witty philosopher and a north-woods troubadour with wing-ed words of pure gold. There was that character, Ed Grant, who tamed a trout so it could live out of water, and then the trout fell in the brook and drowned. Or that other character, what's-his-name, who rowed a boat so fast the friction on the water set it afire. Did I tell you about Lem Holden, up at Umsaskasooskus Lake, who had a boat powered by porcupines that worked a treadmill? No end to the things those fellows could think up! But they weren't "registered." You didn't need a "license" to be a guide.

Fact is, hunting and fishing licenses had been in effect only a few years. They came about at the time the "meatman" was eliminated. When lumbering became Maine's big business and the choppers began to "let daylight into the swamps," the big north woods became something more than back country. Lumber camps with two or three hundred men in residence were set up, and they remained remote and often isolated from first snow to spring thaw. Food was teamed in before snow fell, and there was no way to replenish provisions. Salt meat, yes, but the only fresh meat would be game from the surrounding forest. So each camp would employ a professional hunter who would keep bear, deer, moose, and caribou hanging in the dingle. Also "jibbers," from the Canadian-French word *gibier* for small game. Rabbits, pa'tridges, raccoons, and porcupines could be used in "beef" stews. These hunters were called "meatmen," and sometimes "camp-hunters." But preservationists and environmentalists had antecedents, and all at once this wholesale use of game animals was deplored. A law ensued that no game could be served in a lumber camp, or in a public eating place. All at once every meatman in Maine was unemployed. Since the same kind of thinking that outlawed the meatman suggested game management and wildlife conservation, leading to a Fish and Game Department at the state house, these meatmen mostly became game wardens. Our first warden force consisted of the finest poachers in the state, and some of the best stories our early registered guides told had to do with this paradoxical pleasantry. There arose during this happy transition the reason for licenses. The cost of a Fish and Game Department, and wardens, should be saddled on the Waltons and Nimrods, not on the taxpayer. The first fishing license I had cost me twenty-five cents. Next came the "combination" license, which cost a dollar and covered both hunting and fishing. A few years later, as bureaucracy grew and the commissioner needed suede sneakers for the wardens, some-body thought of licensing the guides. One little thing, another little thing, and thus grows the gourd. Nobody thought that this was like penalizing a poet, or killing a goose for the golden eggs, or stealing from the poor box. It was a foolish bureaucratic deci-sion, but the "Registered Maine Guide" became a fact rather than a legend, a myth, and an asset. He became a victim, and before he could tell lies in the evening he had to pay five dollars for a license. My first guide's license cost five dollars, and I kept pay-ing five dollars every year for a long time, and I never guided anybody.

This is the important thing about this story. The five dollars that made me a Registered Guide included the privilege of hunt-ing and fishing, so the bite was small and the matter was a "little thing." Such a little thing, indeed, that many hunters and fish-ers bought guides' licenses—not to hunt and fish, and not to guide, but because it was a whimsical honor to be a Registered Maine Guide, and at five bucks a painless way of belonging to an esoteric society of good fellows. Since I never guided, the only value I ever received from my fee was to flourish the card and make an impression. I was in the Jägerhaus at Esslingen am Neckar in Germany one time, and flashed my Maine guide's license, and I wouldn't want any finer hospitality than that which ensued. But when the guide's fee was increased to twenty-five dollars a year, I stopped being a Registered Maine Guide. I can get waited on at the Boston Athenaeum for a smaller fee than that.

How about my late pal Alonzo Harold Garcelon? We called him Gus, and he was a practicing dentist in Augusta. He was also Chairman of the Maine Dental Health Department, and a big wheel in the affairs of the dental school at Tufts College. He also became President of the National Rifle Association. He was also a Registered Maine Guide and explained that he bought a license every year "for cosmetic reasons." Gus never guided anybody, and sometimes when he didn't feel like baking the biscuits or poling the canoe, he'd hire a guide. To Gus, and to so very many more of us, being a real "Registered Maine Guide" was a freemasonry of achievement, better than being a Kentucky Colonel and much better than service in the Swiss Guard at the Vatican.

The beauty of the Maine guide, if stated plainly, was that it didn't amount to a hoot in a hollow or a hole in the snow—which was what made it precious. Nobody needed a guide's license if he wanted to guide—he just "took a friend fishing." But a fellow did need a guide's license if he meant to tell tall tales—stretchers—around a campfire to a bunch of paying customers from Westchester County. Maine's officialdom, settled serenely in state house salubrity, had so lost touch with the true State o' Maine that the guides were demoted from their rightful dignity and honor into the flatland category of taxable assets. The price for a guide's license was increased every time the commissioner went to coffee break, and right now stands at seventy-five dollars. Not only that, but before a license is issued, the applicant has to take and pass an examination replete with double-talk and extraneity. There is no requirement whatever that a new-day guide must be able to put butter on a baked potato or mix a hot buttered rum. Worse than that, there are no questions to test his narrative skills, his veracity, and his way of saying ayeh. At seventy-five dollars all the cosmetic reasons pale. Nobody, today, keeps a guide's license because he feels like "belonging." The jokers who run these white-water rafting trips, a new breed in Maine born of new ideas, plunk down their money, but it's a sad fact that no white-water guide yet has contributed a single sentence to the literature and folklore of the real, true, and honest five-dollar guide of the days that were. Talk about diminishing returns!

Have you heard what happened to my ancient friend Flats Jackson? Flats had a Registered Guide's license for years, and used it out of a set of sporting camps he owned on Spencer Stream. Spencer Stream was excellent trout water, but his guests could wade along the banks and didn't need guide service. When hunting season opened, Flats made a specialty of guiding baseball players from the Boston Red Sox. He liked to have them come three at a time, as that made four hands for cribbage, and before each party arrived Flats would have their deer dressed out and hanging in the icehouse. Each party would stay three or four days, and then another party would arrive. Nobody that I know of ever accused Flats of being a poacher, except the game wardens. But they couldn't prove it, and should have held their tongues. Every spring Flats and his wife, Bubbles, would drive down to Florida for spring training, and almost every year the Boston newspapers would have a picture of the Red Sox training dugout, and there would be Flats and Bubbles smiling as if they owned the team, but the real owner, Mr. Yawkey, would be in the picture, too. As time ran along, Flats and Bubbles opened a hot dog stand next to the practice diamond. There wasn't a base-ball player in either league that didn't know Flats and Bubbles. When training camp broke up and the Red Sox headed north, everybody would say, "So long! See you for deer hunting!"

The State of Maine should have paid Flats, instead of soaking him five dollars to guide. Come fall, when the baseball players began to arrive, there would be a small ceremony about hunt-ing. Each sport knew Flats had a deer for him, but if by some uncanny chance a shortstop should shoot his own, it didn't mat-ter. In cool weather a deer will hold over. So Flats would put his sports on stumps up on Eustis Ridge and then circle down by the highway and "do a drive." If he started deer up the hill, all to the good. So one fall Flats had a right fielder and two left-handed pitchers on stumps, and as he came down by the high-way he chanced onto a predicament. A hunter in another party had collapsed from a heart attack, and was stretched out on the road by his automobile, blank-eyed and panting, gun still clutched in his hands, and in great need of attention. Flats was, is, a broad-shouldered man, able, so he scooped this fellow up, gun and all, shoved him in the back seat of the car, backed around, and headed hell-bent for help in Stratton, or Kingfield, and maybe all the way down to the hospital at Farmington.

Flats got the fellow through all right, and he survived. But when they lifted the hunter out of the back seat, he was still holding his rifle in his hands, and a game warden stepped up and arrested Flats for operating a vehicle on a public highway with a loaded gun. It's a fact. Maine law forbids hunting from an automobile, and a loaded gun is prima facie evidence. So Flats was paraded before the beak and he paid a fine of a hundred dollars and costs. It all happened so fast he was back on Eustis Ridge while his baseball players were still sitting on their stumps. The warden, naturally, smiled a foolish smile because the boys had been watching Flats for a long time, hoping to catch him in an unlawful moment. Now they had him and there was rejoicing, and Flats's guide's license was automatically suspended.

No matter that on the following Tuesday the Boston *Post*, the Boston *Globe*, and the Boston *Herald* had front-page pictures of three Red Sox baseball players and the beautiful bucks they had "bagged" in the deep Maine wilderness. No matter that Flats had his picture in the Lewiston *Sun*, the Portland *Press Herald*, and the Bangor Daily *News* as the alert Maine guide who saved the life of a prominent businessman from Noank, Connecticut. What mattered was that the alert game warden had finally caught poor Flats. Flats, on the hoof, was worth in free publicity much more in one day than the state would pay a game warden in a year. One little thing at a time, and it builds up.

But a license to guide and the act of guiding were not then too closely related. Flats had to wait three years before his guide's license was restored, but he kept on guiding—in a way. He knew that a game warden would be hiding behind every tree and he had to keep his nose clean. So when he took his ballplayers up on Eustis Ridge and put them on stumps he would carry a frying pan. While he scouted the puckerbrush, hoping to drive some deer towards his sports, he would bang the frying pan on a tree every rod or so and shout, "I'm cookin'—I'm not guidin'!" This was true, and any warden with average sense knows a cook from a guide.

But while the wardens out in the woods had average sense, the dunderheads in the state house priced the Registered Maine

Guide out of style. One or two guides, maybe, went on lecture tours or got teaching jobs at Harvard, but their spirit was dampened and it's sad when a man realizes his talents are no longer appreciated. If you find a capable Maine guide today, he'll disappoint you. He'll probably tie on your smelt hindside to, and start his fire with fatwood from L. L. Bean. And if he tries to tell you a Maine woods story, he'll garble it all up as if it had been edited for *Reader's Digest*. So you can say that Maine would be Maine today if they'd left the guides' fee at five dollars. Or, to start at the beginning, if we'd clobbered Ralph O. Brewster at the polls when he suggested we take in tourists overnight.

50 Our Last Thanksgiving

Oh! It's two cents a mile on the B&M,
You ride with a smile on the B&M

When Charley Miller (see VACATIONLAND STUFF, about Charley Miller) was doing his publicity stunts to gain free advertising for Maine's advantages and scenic attractions, this jingle of the Boston and Maine Railroad was on just about every New England radio station. That is, Charley could be sent from Bangor, where he had a restaurant, down to Boston and back for less than a ten-spot in train fare. His baggage was checked on his ticket, so that rode free—his tent, his frypan, his bedroll. He cooked his own meals. He slept in his tent (or in jail if he had trouble with a cop) and there was no hotel bill. The Maine Department of Hoopla paid him guide's wages, and his fines if he got any, and in this inexpensive way Charley would garner ten or fifteen pages of free Sunday Supplement publicity that couldn't be bought otherwise at any price. Let us look at Charley Miller as he gets his "stunt" ready in this Philadelphia *Bulletin* photograph:

Philadelphia *Bulletin*

Observe, please, the utter simplicity of the *mise en scène*. This is no Hollywood extravaganza, no *Birth of a Nation* diorama. Charley has just what any Maine woodsman would have—shelter and gear, and warm clothes. He is not about to entertain any nabobs and pontiffs. He's just a honest down-Mainer come to the big city to go and see the Sportsman's Show (opening Monday!). Notice Charley's hat. That hat, leather with flaps, was designed by Ortho Bean, brother to L. L. Bean, and offered to the public as the cap worn to the Arctic by Explorer Donald B. MacMillan in 1925. The things were indestructible, and back at Bangor Charley used to wear his while cooking in his restaurant as well as on the trail when he guided sports. If you look back of Charley, by the parked automobile of the *Bulletin* photographer, you'll see two duffle bags in which Charley has the things he'll need to serve a full-course roast-beef dinner to the civic leaders, police, press corps, and other guests invited by the Sportsman's Show management—all of whom will be a big surprise to Charley, who will protest that he is just down for a few days to see the show.

Let us now look at Picture No. 2 in this informative sequence:

Maine State Archives

Notice all the people who are being paid scale. Times have changed—Charley Miller has made the long hike over the divide and somebody else has taken over his restaurant. The easy-going and competent Maine Development Commission has been re-evaluated and named the Department of Economic Development at great expense, and instead of a bunch of seat-warmers to think things up, we now have experts and specialists. Not only that, but the whole state house has been put on the multiple-choice system, thought up by Freddie Payne. Freddie was a used-car salesman from Waldoboro who ran for governor on a promise of lower taxes and extreme economy. As he turned from taking the oath of office he announced his plan for a 4 percent sales tax. Then he organized the Department of Public Employment, which hired people for state house jobs. To make this work easier for all, every time anybody was hired there had to be ten of them. If a man up in the office of counting blueberry pickers needed a stenographer, advertising was placed, examinations scheduled, and an address printed for receiving testimonials. In due time ten stenographers would be hired, and then the department had to find nine other men who needed a stenographer. Right after that, Freddie said the 4 percent would have to be raised to five. So here is the picture of all the people who got together, donned costumes, and performed in a small Thanksgiving stunt that Charley Miller could have done at two cents a mile.

This is great stuff to show people who ask if Maine has changed very much.

It is good history that the "First Thanksgiving" was not held at Plymouth by the Pilgrims. In 1607, fourteen years before the Pilgrims held their big feast, the colonists at Popham were grateful for their safe crossing of the Atlantic and they rejoiced in a "service of thanksgiving." The Popham colonists were not dissenters, like the Pilgrims, but had an appointed chaplain who was an Episcopalian priest—the Rev. Richard Seymour. Fr. Seymour conducted. One of the publicity experts, name of Reggie Bouchard, of the newly funded Department of Economic Development, heard about this waif of history, and decided Maine needed to be better known the world around as the original turkey-day instigator. That's how-come all the people in the picture congregated for the big re-enactment of the First Thanksgiving. Now we can look at Reggie's picture, for which he received kudos at the time and was hailed as a benefactor:

Courtesy Associated Press

So what has happened to Maine?

There were no women in the Popham colony. A hundred and twenty men, recruited in England to establish a fisheries station "at The Maine," were to be joined later by spouses, but the colony failed and no further colonization ensued. In short, the accepted version of the Plymouth Thanksgiving persisted and colored the Maine version with unhistorical femininity. Nice touch, but kitsch.

Now, regard the Indians! There were no Indians at the first Maine Thanksgiving. The Pemaquids were in the vicinity, and there had been meetings of Reds and Whites, but both mistrusted the other. Nahanada, a sachem of the Pemaquids, had been to England and spoke English, and he had asked the colonists to refrain from any show of force that might cause his braves to react. On the day of the Thanksgiving exercises, Nahanada had withdrawn his people from the area. Fr. Seymour had a completely white congregation as he prayed.

Not only that, but the Indians you see in Reggie's photograph are interesting by themselves. The one in the feathered bonnet, reaching for a lobster, was, and is, Chief Bruce Poolaw, who, for many years, has been resident at the Penobscot Tribe island at Old Town. He keeps "The Teepee," a gift and souvenir shop just at the end of the bridge to the island. He is not a Penobscot, and if any Indians had been at the Popham Thanksgiving they would not have been Penobscots anyway. Chief Bruce Poolaw is a Kiowa Indian from Oklahoma, a tribe with quite a stirring history that was awarded United States citizenship in 1901. For one thing, the Kiowas came closer to a written language than any other Amerinds, and were outstanding among the Plains Indians. At one time, because of clashes, many Kiowas were moved from their Oklahoma lands to Florida. Chief Bruce Poolaw had a brother who was a member of the United States Congress from Oklahoma. The Chief, when he came to Maine, married a Penobscot princess, and has remained as somebody to see if you visit Indian Island.

And for another thing, Chief Poolaw would readily point out, if anybody asked about it, that his elaborate Plains Indian feather war bonnet would not have been seen at Popham if any Indian had arrived for the exercises. In 1607 Chief Nahanada of the Pemaquids was probably wearing a stylish suit made for him by a London tailor. The Pemaquids had known about Europeans for some four hundred years, and at times Chief Nahanada would walk about Pemaquid swinging an ebony cane such as dandies affected along the Thames.

This photograph of Maine's First Thanksgiving was distributed nationwide from the Boston office of Associated Press Photos on the 13th of November, 1964, and was used by most of the member newspapers. It also got good play on television, which was then coming along fine.

That's all at this time.